Communications
in Computer and Information Science   386

Juan A. Botía
Juan Antonio Álvarez García
Kaori Fujinami   Paolo Barsocchi
Till Riedel (Eds.)

Evaluating AAL Systems Through Competitive Benchmarking

International Competitions and Final Workshop, EvAAL 2013
July and September 2013
Proceedings

 Springer

Volume Editors

Juan A. Botía
Universidad de Murcia, Spain
E-mail: juanbot@um.es

Juan Antonio Álvarez García
University of Seville, Spain
E-mail: jaalvarez@us.es

Kaori Fujinami
Tokyo University of Agriculture and Technology, Tokyo, Japan
E-mail: fujinami@cc.tuat.ac.jp

Paolo Barsocchi
ISTI Institute of CNR, Pisa, Italy
E-mail: paolo.barsocchi@isti.cnr.it

Till Riedel
Karlsruhe Institute of Technology, Germany
E-mail: riedel@teco.edu

ISSN 1865-0929   e-ISSN 1865-0937
ISBN 978-3-642-41042-0   e-ISBN 978-3-642-41043-7
DOI 10.1007/978-3-642-41043-7
Springer Heidelberg New York Dordrecht London

Library of Congress Control Number: 2013948093

CR Subject Classification (1998): C.4, C.3, K.4, I.2.10, I.4, C.2, C.5, H.4, J.3, J.2

Typesetting: Camera-ready by author, data conversion by Scientific Publishing Services, Chennai, India

Printed on acid-free paper

Springer is part of Springer Science+Business Media (www.springer.com)

Preface

In the last decade, we have experienced a paradigm shift in the way we use computers. We have moved from a world of personal computers to a world of many different kinds of smaller devices. Many of those devices are deployed everywhere, i.e., sensors and actuators. Others are hand-held mobile devices with unthinkable computing capabilities years ago, i.e., smart phones and tablets. Software is also experiencing significant changes, from single non smart applications to a myriad of smart services accessible anytime and anywhere. Ambient-assisted living (AAL), a research program created within the EU devoted to fostering the development of new ICT technologies for independent living of the elderly and disabled, can be seen as a natural consequence of such new scenario.

To enable the adoption of AAL solutions by industry, both means for validation of systems and benchmarks for the comparison of ALL solutions and platforms, are a must. The EvAAL (Evaluation of AAL Systems through Competitive Benchmarking) competition was born of this aim. It is an annual international contest promoted by the AALOA association. Its main goal is to assess, on the participant AAL platforms, the level of autonomy, independent living, and quality of life they deliver to end users. This goal is enabled through the establishment of suitable benchmarks and evaluation metrics.

This book is a compilation of papers describing the systems participating in the third edition of the EvAAL competition. The first edition in 2011 was centered on indoor localization. The second edition in 2012 included a track on activity recognition. This third edition in 2013 maintained both tracks. The *Indoor Localization and Tracking for AAL* track was held in Madrid, Spain, during July 15, 2013. The *Activity Recognition for AAL* track was also held in Spain, Valencia, during July 8–12, 2013. The first track included seven different participants and the second track comprised four participants. A final workshop to sum up and discuss the results was celebrated in conjunction with the AAL Forum in September 2013 in Norrköping, Sweden. We sincerely hope the reader finds this compilation interesting for getting acquainted with the state of the art in two basic tasks of ambient intelligence in general and AAL systems in particular: indoor location and activity recognition.

We would like to thank everybody who made this volume of proceedings possible. Firstly, we thank the Organizing Committees of this initiative and the AALOA institution for its support. Obviously, we also want to thank the authors for their effort in preparing this set of high-quality papers. Special thanks must also be given to the two living labs that hosted the (1) Indoor Localization and Tracking and (2) the Activity Recognition events: Polytechnic University of Madrid's Living Lab and the CIAmI Living Lab, respectively. And finally, a special mention must be made of our sponsors: the UniversAAL Project, meGha, Asus Xtion and joiiup.

June 2013   Juan A. Botía

Organization

The third edition of the EvAAL competition was divided into two different events: the Indoor Localization and Tracking event and the Activity Recognition event. Both events were held in Spain. The first was organized by the Living Lab of the Polytechnic University of Madrid. The second was organized by the CIAmI Living Lab in Valencia.

Committees

General Chairs:

Juan Carlos Augusto	Middlesex University, UK
Stefano Chessa	University of Pisa, Italy, (as deputy of Francesco Furfari, CNR-ISTI, Italy)

Indoor Localization and Tracking Chairs:

Till Riedel	Karlsruhe Institute of Technology, Germany
Paolo Barsocchi	CNR-ISTI, Italy

Activity Recognition Chairs:

Kaori Fujinami	Tokyo University of Agriculture and Technology, Japan
Juan Antonio Álvarez García	University of Seville, Spain

Local Committee Chairs:

Dario Salvi	Polytechnic University of Madrid, Spain
Juan Pablo Lázaro	TSB Soluciones Tecnologicas, Spain
Filippo Cavallo	Scuola Superiore S. Anna, Italy

Publication Chair:

Juan A. Botía	University of Murcia, Spain

Publicity Chair:

Francesco Potortì	ISTI-CNR, Italy

Dataset Management Chair:

Stefano Chessa	Pisa University, Italy

Software Tools:

Alejandro Medrano	Polytechnic University of Madrid, Spain

Financial Chairs:

Rose Lai	ITRI, Taiwan
Morgen Chang	ITRI, Taiwan
Axel Sikora	University of Applied Sciences Offenburg, Germany
Jesús Bermejo	Telvent, Spain

Program Committee of the Indoor Loalization and Tracking Track

Adriano Moreira	University of Minho, Portugal
Ivan Martinovic	University of Oxford, UK
Binghao Li	University of New South Wales, Australia
Maurizio Bocca	University of Utah, USA
Stefan Knauth	Stuttgart University, Germany
Francesco Potortì	CNR-ISTI, Italy
Michele Girolami	CNR-ISTI, Italy
Filipe Meneses	University of Minho, Portugal
Bruno Andò	University of Catania, Italy
Axel Sikora	University of Applied Sciences Offenburg, Germany
Moustafa Youssef	University of Science and Technology Alexandria, Egypt
Marco Zuniga	Delft University of Technology, The Netherlands
Wilhelm Stork	Institute for Information Processing Technologies, Germany
Steffen Meyer	Fraunhofer Institute for Integrated Circuits IIS, Germany
Philippe Canalda	Femto-ST Institute UMR CNRS, France

Program Committee of the Activity Recognition Track

Alessio Micheli	University of Pisa, Italy
Cecilio Angulo	Universitat Politècnica de Catalunya - BarcelonaTech, Spain
Stefano Chessa	University of Pisa, Italy
Kazuya Murao	Kobe University, Japan
Roozbeh Jafari	University of Texas at Dallas, USA
Luis Miguel Soria	University of Seville, Spain
Fahim Kawsar	Alcatel-Lucent, Belgium
Susanna Pirttikangas	University of Oulu, Finland
Sozo Inoue	Kyushu Institute of Technology, Japan

Jin-Hyuk Hong   Carnegie Melon University, USA
Mitja Lustrek   Jozef Stefan Institute, Slovenia
Wenwei YU   Chiba University, Japan
Roberta Giannantonio   Telecom Italia, Italy

Sponsoring Institutions

The EvAAL competition is hosted by AALOA and sponsored by the following
organizations:
The EU Funded UniversAAL Project.
meGha
Asus Xtion
joiiup

Table of Contents

An Improved Saliency for RGB-D Visual Tracking and Control Strategies for a Bio-monitoring Mobile Robot

Nevrez Imamoglu[1], Zhixuan Wei[2], Huangjun Shi[3], Yuki Yoshida[1],
Myagmarbayar Nergui[1], Jose Gonzalez[1], Dongyun Gu[3],
Weidong Chen[2], Kenzo Nonami[1], and Wenwei Yu[1]

[1] Graduate School of Engineering, Chiba University, Chiba, Japan
{nevrez.imamoglu,jose.gonzalez}@chiba-u.jp, chikiny@me.com,
myagaa@graduate.chiba-u.jp, {nonami,yuwill}@faculty.chiba-u.jp
[2] Institute of Robotics and Intelligent Information Processing, Department of Automation,
Shanghai Jiao Tong University, Shanghai, People's Republic of China
zhixuan.wei@gmail.com, wdchen@sjtu.edu.cn
[3] Department of Biomedical Engineering, Shanghai Jiao Tong University,
Shanghai, People's Republic of China
hjshi84@sjtu.edu.cn, gudongyun@163.com

Abstract. Our previous studies demonstrated that the idea of bio-monitoring home healthcare mobile robots is feasible. Therefore, by developing algorithms for mobile robot based tracking, measuring, and activity recognition of human subjects, we would be able to help impaired people (MIPs) to spend more time focusing in their motor function rehabilitation process from their homes.

In this study we aimed at improving two important modules in these kinds of systems: the control of the robot and visual tracking of the human subject. For this purpose: 1) tracking strategies for different types of home environments were tested in a simulator to investigate the effect on robot behavior; 2) a multi-channel saliency fusion model with high perceptual quality was proposed and integrated into RGB-D based visual tracking.

Regarding the control strategies, results showed that, depending on different types of room environment, different tracking strategies should be employed. For the visual tracking, the proposed saliency fusion model yielded good results by improving the saliency output. Also, the integration of this saliency model resulted in better performance of RGB-D based visual tracking application.

Keywords: Multi-channel saliency fusion, RGB-D visual tracking, particle filter, PID control, robot control.

1 Introduction

In our previous studies, we were able to detect and track human subjects using the software development kit (SDK) of Microsoft Kinect sensor (Fig.1), which includes an RGB camera and a Depth sensor. We also implemented different methods that allowed us to improve the accuracy of the skeletal points extracted from the color and depth images of the Kinect [1]. Then, using this information we were able to track the

J.A. Botía et al. (Eds.): EvAAL 2013, CCIS 386, pp. 1–12, 2013.
© Springer-Verlag Berlin Heidelberg 2013

subject in real environments, measure his joint trajectories (Fig.2), and recognize different activities [1]. A Hidden Markov Model (HMM) [1, 2] was applied on human joint angle data for activity recognition with a higher recognition rate compared to other tested classification models [1].

One of the main tasks of the mobile robot is the detection and tracking of the subject. Once a subject is detected, the robot will move towards him avoiding any obstacles on the way and keeping the subject at the middle of the visual field. Certainly, in order to avoid any bumping accidents the robot always keeps a fixed distance from the subject. However when the robot is moving, tracking the subject becomes more difficult due to random environmental changes or the vibration caused by the robot's motion or sensor rotation [2]. Hence, improvements both for the robot's motion behavior and visual subject tracking are required in order for it to work in the real daily living environment.

Fig. 1. Robot used in the studies

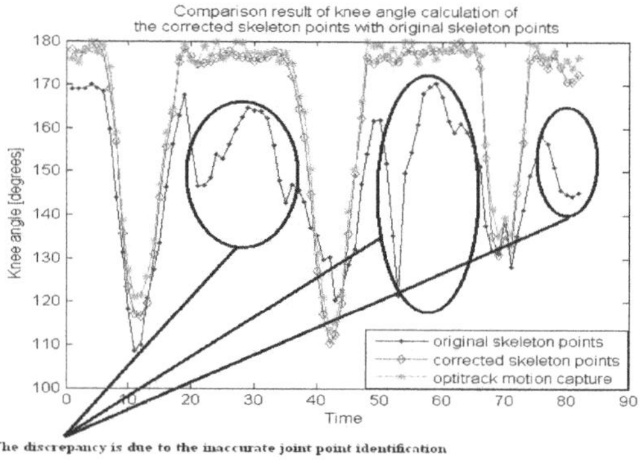

Fig. 2. Comparison result of knee angle calculation of the corrected skeleton points with original skeleton points

Therefore in this study, 1) tracking strategies for different types of home environments were tested in a simulator to observe the effect on robot behavior; 2) an improved multi-channel saliency fusion model was proposed, especially for high perceptual quality saliency models to decrease the irrelevant salient regions. This new saliency model, which utilizes principle component analysis (PCA) [3] and multi-channel pulse-coupled neural network (m-PCNN) [4], was integrated into an RGB-D particle filter based visual tracking [5-7] application to observe whether the performance improved or not.

The paper is organized as follows: In section 2, the approach to test and analyze the control effect on the robot in different conditions is given. Section 3 explains the proposed multi-channel saliency fusion model and its integration for visual tracking based on particle filter model. Experiment setup and the results are given in Section 4, and then following concluding remarks are stated.

2   Investigating the Effect of Tracking Strategies in Simulation

In our previous works, the system has not been tested in different types of indoor environment, for example different size of the room, the density of furniture that could be the obstacle for mobile robot, the room containing dead-end or not, etc. (Fig.3). It is very important to test different scenarios to improve the tracking strategies of the bio-monitoring robot in the real daily living environment.

The effect of these problems can't be separated and observed easily on real environment, thus we employed a Mobile Robot Simulator (Webots7.1.0, CYBERBOTICS) to test different tracking strategies for different types of rooms. Similarly to our past work, we used a reactive controller to enable the robot to avoid obstacles while following the subject using a position PID control. For this study we compared two tracking strategies for two different simulated home environments. In Strategy A the robot keeps tracking the target without stopping. On the other hand, in strategy B, the robot doesn't move until the target goes outside of the camera's visual field. In both cases a position PID control was used. We compared these two strategies in a large room (8m*8m) environment, and a small room environment (4m*4m) as shown in Fig.3. Each trial lasted for 60 seconds.

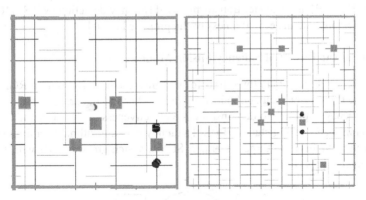

Fig. 3. A small environment(left) and a large environment(right) with obstacles and robots

3   Visual Tracking

The work we have done until now had relied mainly on the data acquired through the Kinect SDK, but a better and more reliable model should be implemented to increase the accuracy of visual tracking. Therefore, considering the computational visual attention (VA) models, based on the visual attention mechanisms of humans, the attentive or salient regions of images with respect to several features (intensity, color, motion, and etc.) could be used to reduce redundant information by giving priority to these salient cues. This will result in better representations of the scene, which could improve visual tracking. Hence, first, we proposed a framework for salient feature channel fusion for saliency approaches to improve the saliency output to decrease irrelevant salient regions.

3.1   Saliency Fusion in Eigenvector Space with an *m*-PCNN

Saliency maps provide useful features by selecting significant parts and reducing the redundant data from the perceived visual scene locally and globally based on the concept of visual attention (VA) mechanism [8-11]. This way, the resultant data can be used for further processing such as detection, segmentation, and data reduction. Saliency computational models take advantage of internal [8] or external [9] modules to identify local relations among salient features or to avoid irrelevant salient regions for better scene representation in the computed saliency maps. Internal approaches have the advantage of being independent of the application and have the ability to utilize space projection, feature extraction, and fusion concepts as a closed approach in an integrated manner. Therefore, in the present paper, we apply an internal approach that aims at; i) local-to-global feature differences with statistical correlations among the feature spaces without any normalization process, and ii) improvement of the uniformity around the salient regions and reduction of irrelevant small salient regions. The proposed model is for saliency conspicuity map fusion using two concepts such as input image transformation relying on principal component analysis [3] and saliency conspicuity map fusion with a multi-channel pulse-coupled neural network [4] with two different recent saliency computational models (i.e. frequency-tuned saliency detection (FTS) [9] and wavelet-transform-based saliency detection (WTS) [10]) separately to demonstrate the effectiveness of the proposed model.

Procedure of the Proposed Saliency Fusion Model

The proposed method inputs three transformed image channels from an RGB image by using the three eigenvectors obtained by PCA. Then, SCMs are generated with the selected saliency approach to demonstrate the effectiveness of the PCA and m-PCNN integration into an existing state-of-the-art saliency map algorithm. As a final step, m-PCNN is used to fuse the three generated SCMs, which are weighted with their respective eigenvalues (Fig.4).

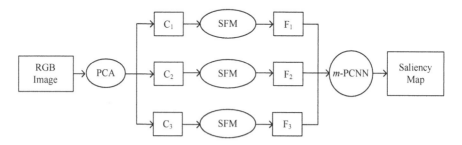

Fig. 4. Flowchart of the proposed saliency fusion model

where C_i is the transformed data in the eigenvector space for each principal component, SFM is the saliency conspicuity map generation, F_i is the SCM, and *m*-PCNN is the fusion model based on the multi-channel pulse-coupled neural network.

Input Image Transformation by PCA

The initial step in the proposed system is to obtain the PCA for an *RGB* input image as in [3] to obtain the respective eigenvalues and eigenvectors. First, a Gaussian filter is applied for smoothing, and then, the *RGB* image is converted to two-dimensional (2D) data by making each R, G, and B channel a raw vector. Then, PCA is applied to the data to obtain eigenvalues and eigenvectors. The first principal component of the eigenvalues and eigenvector pairs has the highest eigenvalue in the set. The transformations for each eigenvector space can be done as in (1) [3]:

$$A_i = (\xi_i^T \times v^T),\qquad(1)$$

where A_i is the transformed data in the eigenvector space based on the ith principal component, v is the zero mean adjusted data, ξ_i is the ith principal eigenvector, and T is the transpose operation. Then, 1D A_i is remapped to 2D C_i data regarding the row and column size of the image, where C_i are the input images for the saliency computation. Obviously, as it can be seen in Fig.5, local and global information content can be controlled with PCA-based representation more practical than with other tools such as internal feature normalization methods [8] or an external assistive segmentation algorithm [9] to enhance the saliency map.

Fig. 5. Sample RGB color images, their respective eigenvector space representations (first, second, and third principal transformations (rows 2–4, columns 1 and 3, top to bottom, respectively), and the respective WTS-based [10] SMCs of each eigenvector space representation (to the right of each transformation image)

Saliency Conspicuity Maps for Each Component

For more detailed information, it is necessary to have SCMs with full resolution. We selected two recent saliency frameworks to integrate the proposed fusion model. The saliency map in [9] (FTS model) computes the SCMs based on the difference between a Gaussian blurred image and the mean value of the image that yields more globally

biased saliency information. The local saliency map of [10] (WTS model) was selected as another modality. It is based on inverse WT (IWT) that avoids low-pass
signals in a multi-scale perspective, thereby providing regional differences from edge
to texture in a more local perspective. FTS and WTS were selected because it is good
to have local-to-global saliency models separately to show the performance of PCA
and m-PCNN-based fusion. The m-PCNN aims to improve the final saliency result by
considering the relations among neighboring pixels during the fusion process, and
there is no need for a CIE Lab color space transformation in either FTS or WTS integration owing to PCA utilization. Therefore, FTS [9] and WTS [10] were adopted for
the proposed model to compute the saliency conspicuity maps of each input channel
separately as in Fig.4. In Fig.5, examples of WTS-based conspicuity maps are computed from the PCA inputs. It can be seen that each eigenvector space has a unique
saliency representation where the third principal components have the most global
saliency information compared to the others.

Fusion by m-PCNN

The next step is to combine all SCMs into a final saliency map. The PCNN can be
regarded as a promising algorithm for information fusion since its usability has been
proven in many image processing applications [4]. In this paper, m-PCNN with autonomous weighting adaptation was applied as the fusion model. The basic idea can be
described by the fact that each input channel behaves as a feeding compartment and
also as a linkage between other input channels as stated in [4]. The formulations for
the structure are given as follows [4]:

$$H_{i,j}^k[n] = e^{-\alpha_H} H_{i,j}^k[n-1] + V_H\left(W * Y_{i,j}^k[n-1]\right) + I_{i,j}^k \tag{2}$$

$$U_{i,j}[n] = \prod_{k=1}^{K}\left(1 + \beta^k H_{i,j}^k[n]\right) \tag{3}$$

$$Y_{i,j}[n] = \begin{cases} 1, & U_{i,j}[n] > T_{i,j}[n-1] \\ 0, & else \end{cases} \tag{4}$$

$$T_{i,j}[n] = e^{-\alpha_T} T_{i,j}[n-1] + V_T Y_{i,j}[n] \tag{5}$$

$$W_{mn} = 1/\left[(m)^2 + (n)^2\right] \tag{6}$$

where $k = \{1,2,3\}$ refers to the input channels, W is the weight matrix (6) in which m
and n—representing the location of the surrounding pixels—are the distances to the
center pixel on the x–y plane, I is the input stimulus, H is the external stimulus from
the feed function (2), U is the output (3) by combining linking structures for each
iteration n, and $Y_{i,j}$ is the fired neuron that is defined by the dynamic threshold T. The
other parameters are assigned as $\alpha_H = 0.001$ (2), $V_H = 15$ (2), $\alpha_T = 0.012$ (5), $V_T = 100$
(5), $\beta_k = \varepsilon_k$ (3), and ε_k is the normalized eigenvalue of the kth eigenvector space where
$\sum \varepsilon_k = 1$ should be satisfied [4]. Initially, $Y_{i,j}$, $U_{i,j}$, and $T_{i,j}$ are all set to zero, and $H_{i,j}^k$ is
initially valued as $I_{i,j}^k$; after the iterations are completed, the square root of U is taken

as the fused final saliency to decrease the high variation during fusion due to modulation. Using the eigenvalues based on the PCA, we can control the weight of each SCM autonomously during fusion where the first input channel has the highest weight, since the SCM will be more representative if it has more local and global information, owing to the high variation in the first eigenvector space. In addition, the surrounding salient region will be more uniform, and noisy small false salient regions will be decreased or removed by the m-PCNN fusion model.

3.2　　Proposed Saliency Model and RGB-D Particle Filter Visual Tracking

Particle filter based visual tracking is not a new approach; for example, the algorithm in [5] showed an adaptive color-based particle filter. The color distribution was taken into account as the observation model, and pixel positions are used for the state space for updating the state of the particles. Then, the use of 3D state space was proposed in [6] where depth was also used as the observation for the particles. Therefore, in our previous experiments, we found out that that a simplified way to integrate depth with 2D state space definition is enough by using depth likelihood feature together with the color distribution to achieve particle filter visual tracking. In addition, Frintrop$et.al.$ [7] defined a component-based descriptor for particle observation based on the salient feature space from the intensity and color channels. Particle weights were updated based the similarity value between the particle observation and reference observation by using the saliency feature space [7]. Therefore, we implemented an efficient algorithm to use i) proposed saliency map model instead of using several saliency feature maps, ii) depth likelihood just as observation rather than including it in state space, and iii) color distribution for particle filter visual tracking.

First, for the subject of interest, reference color distribution [5] and depth value is obtained from RoI to be tracked that is defined by an ellipse. The state space for each particle should be defined as below [5-6]:

$$\mathbf{s}_t = \left\{ x_t, y_t, \dot{x}_t, \dot{y}_t, Hx_t, Hy_t, \theta_t \right\} \tag{7}$$

where x, y represents the position of each particle and centroid of the ellipse to obtained the observation color probability density function (pdf) of particles followed by their velocity, and Hx and Hy are half axes values of ellipse with orientation θ [5]. Then, based on this state space, particles' state update definition over time is achieved by a first order motion model [5, 7].

To find the similarity between the reference color pdf and particles' observations, the Bhattacharyya cooefficient (8) can be used to calculate likelihood of the particles as below [5]:

$$\rho[p,q] = \sum p[n]q[n] ; \quad n \in \left\{ 1, ..., N \right\} \tag{8}$$

The next step is to find the depth likelihood map and saliency map to improve the particle update criteria where the update formulation is given below:

$$w_t = N\left(w_{t-1}c_t d_t s_t\right) \tag{9}$$

where $N(.)$ is the normalizing function to make the sum of weights to 1, w is the particle weight and c is the color likelihood for each particle, d is the depth based particle elimination weight in which d is 1 if the particle inside the segmented depth subject estimation, otherwise 0, and s is the saliency value color scene at the particle position.

Depth likelihood map is generated by a Gaussian function with the depth value obtained from the previous state of the tracked subject so the particles out of subject boundaries can be avoided during new state estimation. With the depth likelihood map, the weights can be kept as the color likelihood update or can be assigned to zero if the particle does not fall on the estimated subject depth region. Thus, particle on the subject boundary can keep on surviving that will increases robustness of the tracking without the necessity of 3D state space usage as used in the work [6]. Moreover, importance of each particle can be controlled by their saliency value since it shows their visibility on the scene. So, the features of attentive particles are less noise free and more reliable compared to the particles at positions without any significance. They are more likely to be observed in the next state too. Hence, with a simple observation and an efficient saliency representation, visual tracking with particle filter defined in 2D state space can achieve good results with RGB-D sensor.

4   Experiments and Results

4.1   Simulation Results for the Robot Control

Two different robot behaviors while tracking were examined in the simulation environment within the two environmental conditions. As stated before, first robot behavior condition keeps the robot tracking without stopping or interruption on the motion. However, for the second case, the robot doesn't move until the target goes outside of defined limits of visual field on the scene. And, for the analysis, we determined an evaluation function as in (10) where L and Ld mean the times of target lost, and its maximum value (4[times] in this research), respectively. V and Vd stand for the standard deviation of vibration of images [pixel]), and its maximal value (10[pixel in this research]). E and Ed mean the error caused by exceeding a distance threshold, and the threshold respectively. From the Fig. 6, it is clear thatthe suitable strategy for large room environment is strategy A. Thereason is that in such an environment, strategy B can't keep effective camera range and must do STOP & GO many times, which could be a major source of camera vibration. From the Fig. 7, it is clear thatthe suitable strategy for a small room environment is strategy B. The reason is that in such small room, strategy B can keep effective camera range and can keep non-movement state. So, it is possible to say that the best strategy for different environment should be different.

$$Value = \frac{L}{Ld}*100 + \frac{V}{Vd}*100 + \frac{E}{Ed}*100 \tag{10}$$

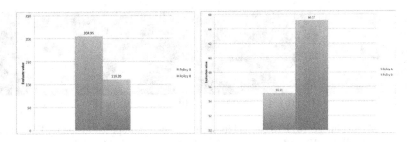

Fig. 6. Results for (left) the large room environment (right) the small room environment

4.2   Evaluation of the Proposed Multi-channel Saliency Fusion Model

Proposed saliency fusion model is evaluated by comparing the consistency of the salient regions with the ground-truth regions labeled by human subjects. In this way, the analysis of the saliency model can be observed quantitatively by the integration of PCA and m-PCNN with the FTS [9] and WTS [10] models. For this purpose, datasets with 5000 images [12] and 1000 images [9] were used for the experiments. The datasets included images and their respective ground truths from various subjects [9, 12]. Saliency models IT [8], SR [11], FTS [9], and WTS [10] were selected for comparison because each model has a unique representation. FTS [9] and WTS [10] were also compared with the proposed model owing to their good performance in full-resolution saliency image quality. The 5000-image dataset of [12] was tested with *precision* (P), *recall* (R), and *F-measure* (Fm) metrics [10]. The commonly used area-under-curve (AUC) performance evaluation [13] was applied to the 1000-image dataset of [9]. The results are shown in Table 1 in favor of proposed model.

Table 1. Quantitative measurementoftheproposedmodel

	(5000 images)			(1000 images)
Method	P	R	F_m	AUC
IT [9]	0.5556	0.5941	0.5640	0.8028
SR [11]	0.5799	0.5412	0.5705	0.8025
FTS [12]	0.5343	0.4470	0.4927	0.8198
WTS [14]	0.6314	0.5949	0.6048	0.8813
Proposed FTS fusion	0.6283	0.6292	0.6076	0.8979
Proposed WTS fusion	0.6444	0.6770	0.6373	0.8925

In Table 1, the improvement over FTS [9] with the current PCA and m-PCNN fusion integration is significant. Further, the same improvements for these measurements are visible for WTS [10] and its integration. This demonstrates that the salient region representing the ground truth increased with some decrease in the irrelevant regions in the final saliency map as shown in the examples in Fig.7. The overall analysis demonstrates the effectiveness of the fusion model with both the FTS and WTS saliency conspicuity map models selected.

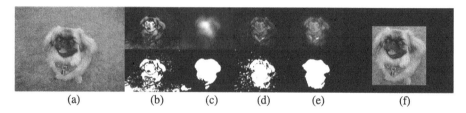

| (a) | (b) | (c) | (d) | (e) | (f) |

Fig. 7. (a) Sample image, (b) FTS [9] and its segmentation (c) proposed fusion for FTS and its segmentation, (d) WTS [10] and its segmentation, (e) proposed fusion for WTS and its segmentation, (f) RoI labeled by the subjects for the 5000-image dataset [12]

4.3   Experimental Results for the Saliency and RGB-D Based Visual Tracking

The experiments on visual tracking based on particle filter with saliency-depth-color observation model was done in dynamic condition such that the subject was moving in any direction in the room and Kinect sensor had rotational motion to keep the subject in the visual filed. First, the color image (Fig.8(a)) from Kinect sensor is used to obtain color distribution of each particle, then depth likelihood map (Fig.8(c)) is computed by depth image (Fig.8(b)) by applying pdf, and finally, we compute saliency map (Fig.8(c)) of the color image with the proposed model. With the all observation, particle weights can be updated to create a more robust visual tracking.

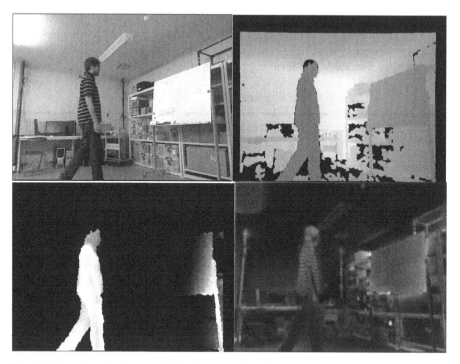

Fig. 8. (a) Sample color image, (b) depth image from Kinect sensor, (c) depth likelihood map obtained from the depth image in (b), (d) saliency map computed by the proposed model

In Fig.9, tracking samples by several frames are given from the experimental recordings. Particles are shown with the ellipse RoI in which ellipse state space is estimated by the weighted average of the particle states. To be able to make an evaluation, we compared particle filter visual tracking in 3 conditions: i) only color observation as in [5], ii) color observation supported by the depth likelihood, and iii) proposed saliency model integration to depth and color observation to update the weights. Each case was tested 20 times in a recorded sequence of video in which the subject was moving and Kinect sensor was rotating.

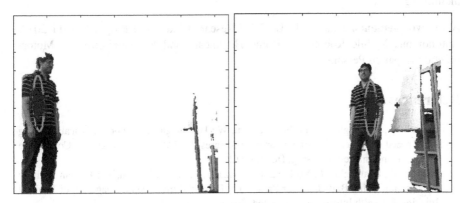

Fig. 9. Sample frames for visual tracking with weighted ellipsoid region on subject body segmented from the depth likelihood

The visual tracking failure condition is defined as the estimated centroid position of the ellipsoid falls on the background region that is not related to the tracked subject. Experimental values for the success and failure numbers are given in Table 2. First condition (only color) was able to complete visual tracking the data 60% of the tests without failure. Second case (color and depth) performed 75% success rate within the 20 tests. On the other hand, using saliency and depth data with color distribution to update weights yielded best tracking success by being able to track 90% of the all tests.

Table 2. Particlefilterbasedvisualtrackingresultsforeachobservationdatacondition

Color Only		Color - Depth		Color – Depth - Saliency	
#Success	#Failure	#Success	#Failure	#Success	#Failure
12	8	15	5	18	2

5   Conclusion

In this study, different modules of a bio-monitoring mobile robot system were examined to develop a reliable structure. First, we investigated tracking strategies for different types of home environments in simulation environment. Then, we proposed a new multi-channel saliency fusion model to integrate saliency and depth data to color based particle filter visual tracking. Experimental analysis demonstrated that adapting new tracking strategies for the robot can be beneficial for different types of room environment. Proposed saliency fusion model yielded promising results by improving the saliency results of two existing state of the arts approach. Also, in the visual tracking experiments, updating the weights of particles with their respective saliency value had improvement on the success rate for the tracking tests. For the future work, the computational efficiency should be improved for real time tracking in real scenario by including human gait recognition and analysis to this system for our ultimate goal which is to develop autonomous mobile home healthcare bio-monitoring robot.

Acknowledgements. Japan JST -US NSF Research Exchange Program, 2011-2013, Autonomous Mobile Robots for Home Healthcare and Bio-monitoring of Motor-function Impaired Persons.

References

1. Nergui, M., Imamoglu, N., Yoshida, Y., Yu, W.: Human gait behavior classification using hmm based on lower body triangular joint features. In: IASTED International Conference on Signal and Image Processing, Honolulu (2012)
2. Nergui, M., Imamoglu, N., Yoshida, Y., Gonzalez, J., Otake, M., Yu, W.: Human Activity Recognition Using Body Contour Parameters Extracted from Depth Images. J. of Medical Imaging & Health Informatics (accepted, 2013)
3. Smith, L.I.: A Tutorial on Principal Component Analysis,
   http://www.cs.otago.ac.nz/cosc453/student_tutorials/principal_components.pdf
4. Wang, Z., Ma, Y.: Medical image fusion using m-PCNN. Information Fusion 9, 176–185 (2008)
5. Paris, S.: Particle Filter Color Tracker. In: Mathworks File Exchange (2011),
   http://www.mathworks.com/matlabcentral/fileexchange/17960-particle-filter-color-tracker
6. Giebel, J., Gavrila, D.M., Schnörr, C.: A Bayesian Framework for Multi-cue 3D Object Tracking. In: Pajdla, T., Matas, J. (eds.) ECCV 2004. LNCS, vol. 3024, pp. 241–252. Springer, Heidelberg (2004)
7. Frintrop, S., Konigs, A., Hoeller, F., Schulz, D.: A Component Based Approach to Visual Person Tracking from a Mobile Platform. Int. J. of Social Robotics 2, 53–62 (2010)
8. Itti, L., Koch, C., Niebur, E.: Model of Saliency-Based Visual Attention for Rapid Scene Analysis. IEEE Trans. on Pattern Analysis and Machine Intelligence 20(11), 1254–1259 (1998)
9. Achanta, R., Hemami, S., Estrada, F., Susstrunk, S.: Frequency-Tuned Salient Region Detection. In: IEEE Int. Conf. CVPR, pp. 1597–1604 (2009)
10. Imamoglu, N., Lin, W., Fang, Y.: A Saliency Detection Model Using Low-Level Features Based on Wavelet Transform. IEEE Trans. on MultiMedia 15(1), 96–105 (2013)
11. Hou, X., Zhang, L.: Saliency Detection: A Spectral Residual Approach. In: IEEE Int. Conf. CVPR, pp. 1–8 (2007)
12. Liu, T., Sun, J., Zheng, N.-N., Tang, X., Shum, H.-Y.: Learning to Detect a Salient Object. In: IEEE Int. Conf. CVPR, pp. 1–8 (2007)
13. Cardillo, G.: ROC curve: compute a Receiver Operating Characteristics curve (2008),
    http://www.mathworks.com/matlabcentral/fileexchange/19950

Efficient Activity Recognition and Fall Detection Using Accelerometers

Simon Kozina, Hristijan Gjoreski, Matjaž Gams, and Mitja Luštrek

Department of Intelligent Systems, Jožef Stefan Institute
Jamova cesta 39, 1000 Ljubljana, Slovenia
{simon.kozina,hristijan.gjoreski,matjaz.gams,
mitja.lustrek}@ijs.si

Abstract. Ambient assisted living (AAL) systems need to understand the user's situation, which makes activity recognition an important component. Falls are one of the most critical problems of the elderly, so AAL systems often incorporate fall detection. We present an activity recognition (AR) and fall detection (FD) system aiming to provide robust real-time performance. It uses two wearable accelerometers, since this is probably the most mature technology for such purpose. For the AR, we developed an architecture that combines rules to recognize postures, which ensures that the behavior of the system is predictable and robust, and classifiers trained with machine learning algorithms, which provide maximum accuracy in the cases that cannot be handled by the rules. For the FD, rules are used that take into account high accelerations associated with falls and the recognized horizontal orientation (e.g., falling is often followed by lying). The system was tested on a dataset containing a wide range of activities, two different types of falls and two events easily mistaken for falls. The F-measure of the AR was 99 %, even though it was never tested on the same persons it was trained on. The F-measure of the FD was 78 % due to the difficulty of the events to be recognized and the need for real-time performance, which made it impossible to rely on the recognition of long lying after a fall.

Keywords: Ambient assisted living, Activity recognition, Fall detection, Machine learning, Rules, Accelerometers.

1   Introduction

The world's population is aging rapidly, threatening to overwhelm the society's capacity to take care of its elderly members. The percentage of persons aged 65 or over in developed countries is projected to rise from 7.5% in 2009 to 16% in 2050 [1]. This is driving the development of innovative ambient assisted living (AAL) technologies to help the elderly live independently for longer and with minimal support from the working-age population [2, 3].

This paper presents a system that recognizes the user's activity and detects falls using wearable sensors. To provide timely and appropriate assistance, AAL systems must understand the user's situation and context, making activity recognition (AR) an

J.A. Botía et al. (Eds.): EvAAL 2013, CCIS 386, pp. 13–23, 2013.
© Springer-Verlag Berlin Heidelberg 2013

essential component [4, 5]. Fall detection (FD) is an important component of many AAL systems because approximately half of the hospitalizations of the elderly are caused by falls [6], fear of falling is an important cause for nursing home admission [7], and "the long lie" (not being able to get up and call for help) is a good predictor of death within six months [8].

AR and FD require a sensor system that observes the user and intelligent software that infers the user's activities from the sensor data [9, 10]. We selected wearable accelerometers as the sensors since they are accurate, inexpensive, can be used both indoors and outdoors, and can be sewn into clothing for minimal intrusiveness. For the AR, we developed an architecture that combines rules to recognize postures, which ensure the behavior of the system is predictable and robust, and classifiers trained with machine learning (ML) algorithms, which provide maximum accuracy in the cases that cannot be handled by the rules. For the FD, rules are used that take into account high accelerations associated with falls and the recognized horizontal orientation (e.g., falling is often followed by lying).

The rest of this paper is organized as follows. An overview of studies related to AR and FD is presented in Section 2. Section 3 gives an overview of the system and the methodology. In Section 4, the sensors and methods used in the AR and FD are described. Section 5 and 6 describe the experimental setup and experimental results, respectively. Section 7 concludes the paper and gives directions for future work.

2   Related Work

AR and FD approaches can be divided into those that use wearable and non-wearable sensors, respectively. The most common non-wearable approach is based on cameras [11]. Although this approach is physically less intrusive for the user compared to one based on wearable sensors, it suffers from problems such as target occlusion, time-consuming processing and privacy concerns. The most mature approach to both AR and FD is probably using wearable accelerometers[12, 13, 14, 15]. There are two common types of wearable-sensor approach that have proven successful: those that use domain knowledge encoded with rules, and those that use machine learning. Most researchers used only one of the two approaches, while our work combines both.

The most common accelerometer-based AR approach uses only ML. Typically a sliding window passes over the stream of sensor data, and the data in each window is classified with one of the known classification methods, such as decision trees (DTs) and support vector machines (SVM). Examples include Kwapisz et al. [12], who used an accelerometer placed on the thigh and compared three classification methods on dynamic activities such as walking, running, and jogging. Ravi et al. [16] used an accelerometer in a mobile phone and tested five classification methods. The results showed that when a given person's data was used for both training and testing, the accuracy was 90%, but when a different person's data was used for the testing, the accuracy dropped to 65%. In our work we never used the same person for training and testing, since the developed model is intended for use by people who were not involved in the training.

An alternative approach to accelerometer-based AR is based on manually created rules. These rules are usually based on features that are calculated from sensor orientations and accelerations. Wu et al. [13] presented an approach in which decision rules are used to recognize activities. Another implementation of such rules was presented by Lai et al. [14], who used six accelerometers, placed on the neck, waist, both wrists and both thighs. The reported accuracy was almost perfect (99.5%), but the number of sensors is excessive for everyday use.

The most common approach to FD use rules that apply thresholds to accelerations and features derived from them, and sometimes consider the activity after a potential fall. Jantaraprim et al. [17] used a triaxial accelerometer worn on the chest; by applying a simple threshold to the acceleration, they detected falls with 98.9 % accuracy. Nguyen, Cho and Lee [19] used a triaxial accelerometer worn on the waist; by applying thresholds to the acceleration, they detected a potential fall and the activity after the fall, resulting in 100 % accurate fall detection. Some researchers used machine learning instead of threshold-based algorithms. Zhang et al. [20] and Shan and Yuan [18] both used a triaxial accelerometer worn on the waist. Using SVM machine learning algorithm on various features derived from accelerations, they detected falls with 96.7 % and 100 % accuracy, respectively. We opted for the rules-based approach, since rules can be understood by humans and are thus less likely to result in unexpected behavior in practice.

3   System Implementation

An overview of the system is shown in Fig. 1. Two accelerometers were attached to the user's chest and thigh. The placement was chosen as a trade-off between the physical intrusiveness and the performance in preliminary tests [11]. The Shimmer sensor platform [21] was chosen because it has a reasonable battery life and compact size, is completely wireless, and has the option to reprogram the sensor based on the user's needs and situation. The platform has a 3-axis accelerometer, uses Bluetooth communication, and has 2 GB of storage, which is enough to store 3 months of sensor data when the frequency of acquisition is 50 Hz. This frequency proved sufficient to capture even the fastest human movement.Additionally, for the purpose of the EvAAL AR competition, a laptop with a long-rangeBluetooth antenna will be used for maximum reliability. In general, though,any kind of Bluetooth device with modest processing capability is sufficient, therefore a smartphone can also be used.

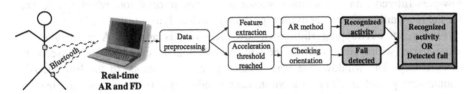

Fig. 1. System overview

The process of the AR and FD is the following.First, the sensors transmit the raw acceleration data over Bluetooth to the processing unit. The data from both sensors is then synchronized, filtered and segmented. Then the flow splits into two. On one side the segmented datais transformed into feature vectors for the AR module, which recognizes the user's activity. On the other side, the FD module checks the acceleration pattern. If a fall pattern is recognized and the predefined acceleration threshold is reached, the user's orientation is checked. If the orientation corresponds to lying (horizontal), a fall is detected. Both the AR and FD modules are evaluating the user's situation every 250 milliseconds which is chosen with accordance to the EvAAL AR competition guidelines. First, the FD module checks for the fall acceleration pattern. If a fall is detected, the system outputs the activity falling; otherwise the AR recognizes and outputs the activity. For instance, if the current system time is denoted with t, the FD module evaluates fall events in the $[t - 2s, t - 1s]$ interval, and the $[t - 1s, t]$ interval is used to check if the orientation of the chest sensor corresponds to lying. If the fall event is detected and the orientation is correct, the reported activity is falling, otherwise the reported activity is computed with the AR module in the $[t - 2s, t]$ interval. The system thus reports the user's activity with a two-second delay.

4   Methods

4.1   Data Preprocessing

The first step in the preprocessing phase is sensor data synchronization. This is necessary when multiple sensors are used, since the data from the sensors is not all received at the same time.

Once the sensor measurements are synchronized, further preprocessing is performed using band-pass and low-pass filters. The acceleration is the sum of the acceleration due to the gravity and the acceleration due to the movement of the sensor (and the person wearing it). The band-pass filter thus has two goals: (1) to eliminate the low-frequency acceleration (gravity) that captures information about the orientation of the sensor with respect to the ground and (2) to eliminate the high-frequency signal components generated by noise, thus preserving the medium-frequency signal components generated by dynamic human motion. The band-pass-filtered data is used for the extraction of features relevant for dynamic activities, such as walking and cycling. The low-pass filter is used to eliminate most of the signals generated by dynamic human motion, preserving the low-frequency component, i.e., gravity [22]. The low-pass-filtered data thus contains sensor orientation information, which is relevant for the recognition of static activities (postures), such as lying, sitting and standing.

Finally, an overlapping sliding-window technique is applied. A window of 2-second size (width) moves across the stream of data, advancing by 250 milliseconds in each step. The window size was selected in correspondence to the EvAAL AR competition guidelines. The data within each window is used to compute the feature vector used for AR described in the next section. The feature vector contains low-pass-filtered features that measure the posture of the body. Additionally, it contains band-pass-filtered features that represent: (1) the motion shape, (2) the motion variance, (3) the motion energy, and (4) the motion periodicity [22]. The feature vector consists of a total of 64 features per sensor.

4.2   Activity Recognition Module

In the AR module, the activities are recognized by a three-level scheme shown in Fig. 2 [23]. On the first level the feature vector is fed into a Random Forest classifier, which is trained to distinguish cycling from the other activities. If an activity is not classified as cycling, the feature vector is passed to the second level, where the activities are recognized by rule-based activity recognition (R-BAR). On this level only features representing average values of low-pass-filtered data are used. The following activities are separated at this level: sitting, lying, bending, and upright posture. If the selected activity is an upright posture, the third level of activity recognition is used to distinguish between standing and walking. The feature vector is again fed into a Random Forest classifier, which is trained to separate these activities. The parameters used for the Random Forest classifier were default ones, as described in Weka's API [24].

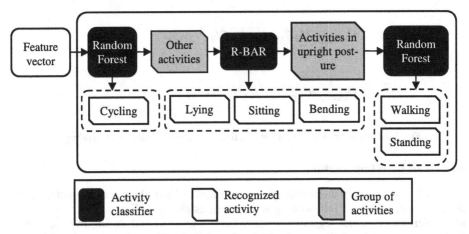

Fig. 2. A three-level AR scheme

R-BAR, used on the second level of the AR, is used for detecting static activities, standing, lying, sitting and bending. Walking, which is a dynamic activity, is merged with its static equivalent, standing. R-BAR uses the orientation of the sensors to recognize posture. The orientation of a sensor is computed with Eq. (1), where i is one of the axes (x, y, or z). Additionally, the orientation is normalized to [0,1] interval.

$$\phi_i = \left(arccos \left(\frac{a_i}{\sqrt{a_x^2 + a_y^2 + a_z^2}} \right) + 1 \right) \cdot \frac{1}{2} \tag{1}$$

The values computed in this way form an orientation vector O=(ϕ_x, ϕ_y,ϕ_z) for one sensor, which is then matched with the set of rules defined by a domain expert as the typical orientations of the sensors for each activity. Figure 3 shows example orientations for three activities (sitting, bending, and upright posture). The structure of the rules in Fig. 3is the following: $O_{activity}=(\phi_{chest,x}, \phi_{chest,y}, \phi_{chest,z}, \phi_{thigh,x}, \phi_{thigh,y}, \phi_{thigh,z})$. For every orientation measurement in vector O, an error is computed using Eq. (2), where d is the absolute difference between the value defined in the rules and the actual measurement. A higher absolute difference d denotes a higher difference between the actual and the typical sensor orientation, resulting in a larger value of the error e.

$$e = \begin{cases} \dfrac{d^4}{0.25^3}; & 0 \le d < 0.25 \\ 3d - 0.5; & 0.25 \le d < 0.5 \\ 1; & 0.5 \le d \end{cases} \qquad (2)$$

The error values form an error vector whose size is the same as that of the orientation vector. These components are summed up in order to obtain the overall error of an activity. Activity with the minimum error is selected as the correct one.

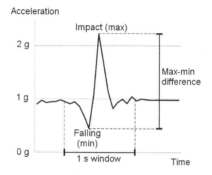

$$O_{sitting}=(^5/_6, ^1/_2, ^1/_2, ^5/_9, ^1/_4, ^1/_2)$$

$$O_{bending}=(^1/_2, ^4/_9, ^3/_4, ^3/_4, ^4/_9, ^1/_2)$$

$$O_{standing}=(^5/_6, ^1/_2, ^1/_2, ^5/_6, ^1/_2, ^1/_2)$$

Fig. 3. Example orientation for three activities: sitting, bending and standing

4.3   Fall Detection Module

A typical acceleration pattern during a fall, measured by a chest accelerometer, is a decrease in acceleration followed by an increase, as shown in Fig. 4. This is because an accelerometer at rest registers 1 g (the Earth's gravity) and during free fall 0 g. When a person starts falling, the acceleration decreases from 1 g to around 0.5 g (perfect free fall is never achieved). Upon the impact with the ground, a short strong increase in the acceleration is measured.

Fig. 4. Acceleration pattern during a fall

To detect falls with a threshold, we used the length of the acceleration vector, which means that we ignored the direction of the acceleration. The minimum and the maximum acceleration within a one-second window were measured. If the difference between the maximum and the minimum exceeded 1 g and the maximum came after the minimum, we declared that a fall had occurred.

We augmented fall detection with the measurement of the person's orientation after a potential fall. We assumed that the acceleration vector $a = [a_x, a_y, a_z]$, which consists of the accelerations along the three axes of the accelerometer, generally points downwards (in the direction of the Earth's gravity). Let z be the axis pointing downwards when the person is standing upright. The angle φ between the acceleration vector and the z axis thus indicates the person's orientation, and was computed as follows:

$$cos\varphi = \frac{a_z}{\sqrt{a_x^2 + a_y^2 + a_z^2}} \tag{3}$$

A person was considered to be oriented upright if $-35° < \varphi < 35°$. This was used for fall detection: if an acceleration fall pattern was detected that exceeded the threshold as described previously, and the orientation in the next second was not upright, we declared that a fall had occurred.

5   Experiments

5.1   Test Scenario

In order to evaluate the AR and FD methods, a complex, 90-minute, scenario was designed in cooperation with a medical expert to capture the real-life conditions of a person's behavior, although it was recorded in a laboratory. The scenario contained several sub-scenarios: walking on a treadmill, cycling on a stationary bicycle, elementary activities such as: sitting, lying, standing, and specialized activities such as: cooking, reading, typing, washing dishes, and scrubbing the floor. A special "fall" sub-scenario was included in order to evaluate the FD method. It contained two non-fall-like events with large accelerations (quickly sitting down and quickly lying down) and two fall events – tripping and falling slowly (fainting).

5.2   Evaluation Metrics

The AR and FD methods were experimentally evaluated on the described test scenario. The evaluation technique for the ML methods, the ones that require training a model, was leave-one-person-out cross validation. This means that a model was trained on the recordings of all the people except one. The remaining person was used to evaluate the model. This procedure was repeated for each person (10 times) and the average performance was measured. This evaluation technique was used because training and testing on the same person's recordings would give overly optimistic results if the intended use of the model is to classify the activities of previously unseen people.

When selecting the measure of performance, we had to decide how to weigh the activities with different total durations, and even more importantly, how to weigh undetected falls compared to falsely detected falls. Both are important: not detecting a fall may endanger a person's health, while false alarms make the system unlikely to be used in real life. We eventually decided to follow the example of the EvAAL AR competition and use the F-measure both for AR and FD, since it weighs all the activities, as well as undetected and falsely detected falls equally. It is defined as a harmonic mean of recall (the percentage of the events recognized as falls/non-falls from all the fall/non-fall events) and precision (the percentage of the events truly being falls/non-falls of all the events recognized as such).

6   Results and Discussion

6.1   Activity Recognition

Table 1 shows the comparison between AR module designed for EvAAL competition and other standard machine learning methods. Using F-measure for the performance evaluator, the AR module outperforms other standard methods from 0.79 percentage points (Random Forest) up to 2.68 percentage points (Decision Tree).

Table 1. EvAAL AR module compared to the other standard classification methods

ML algorithm	Decision Tree	Naive Bayes	Random Forest	EvAAL AR
F-measure	96.36%	97.93%	98.25%	99.04%
Precision	96.53%	97.75%	97.90%	98.85%
Recall	96.19%	98.11%	98.61%	99.22%

To obtain a better insight into which activities are misclassified, the confusion matrices for all the algorithms are presented in Fig 5.

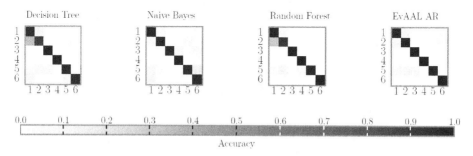

Fig. 5. Confusion matrices for all compared algorithms. Activity legend: 1 – walking, 2 – standing, 3 – sitting, 4 – lying, 5 – bending, 6– cycling.

Decision Tree and Random Forest classifiers have problems separating between walking and standing activities. This is probably due to the fact, that both activities have similar average values when computed over a time window. Naive Bayes classifier however fails at accurately recognizing cycling and walking. Although AR module developed for EvAAL has misclassifiedsome standing and walking activities, it still outperforms other methods.

6.2   Fall Detection

The FD results (shown in Table 2) show that the first event – tripping (quick uncontrolled fall) is detected each time (15 out of all 15 events). The next event, i.e., fainting, is detected 13 out of 15 times. The next two events are the non-fall events that are difficult to distinguish from the fast falls because of the huge acceleration. Because the FD module also checks the user's orientation after a potential fall (huge acceleration), it was able to distinguish quickly sitting on the chair from the classical falls (only 1 false detection). However, the problem still exists in the event in which the user quickly lies into the bed (13false detections). For correct recognition of this event, additional information about the user is needed, e.g., user's location.

Table 2. Fall detection results

Events	Detected/All		Recall	Precision	F-measure
Tripping	15/15				
Fainting	13/15				
Quickly lying	13/15		**93.33%**	**66.67%**	**77.78%**
Quickly sitting	1/15				
Other	0				

The overall performance of the FD method shows that 93.3% of the fall events were detected (recall value), 66.7% of all the fall detections were actually falls (precision value), giving a final F-measure of 77.8%.

7   Conclusion

This paper presented an approach for AR and FD that emphasizes robustness and real-time performance: it combines human-understandable rules with classifiers trained with ML. The rules can classify postures (static activities) quite accurately, and they ensure that the behavior of the system is as predictable as possible and that nothing unforeseen occurs when it is deployedin practice. However, since constructing understandable and accurate rules for dynamic activities is difficult or even impossible, ML classifiers are used for these activities. On the other hand, the FD method first recognizes the high acceleration fall pattern and then checks the user's orientation. If the orientation corresponds to lying, a fall is detected; otherwise the recognized activity from the AR module is used as system's output.

The system was tested on a dataset containing a wide range of activities, two different types of falls and two events easily mistaken for falls. The F-measure of the AR was 99 %, which is very good for only two accelerometers and leave-one-person-out cross-validation. It can partly be attributed to our AR architecture and partly to the high quality of the dataset, since great care was taken to include only technically perfect data (no corrupted signals or incorrect labels). The F-measure of the FD was 78 %, which is not so good, but acceptable given the difficulty of the task. The main problem was mistaking lying down quickly for a fall, but could hardly be avoided without knowing that the event took place on a bed (impossible with accelerometers only) and without being able to observe the lying after a suspected fall for some time (impossible due to the emphasis on real-time performance).

We are currently working on the ergonomics aspect of our system. The two accelerometers are presently attached to the user with elastic straps, but we plan to sew them into clothing, if this can be done without significantly decreasing the accuracy due to less secure attachment. It appears that there is not much room for improvement of the AR accuracy, but the FD accuracy is less satisfactory. Therefore we plan to investigate approaches to improve this, both with additional sensors or by allowing more time to determine the context of a potential fall, and by improvements of the FD method only.

References

1. United Nations 2009, World population ageing, Report (2009)
2. Bourouis, A., Feham, M., Bouchachia, A.: A new architecture of a ubiquitous health monitoring system: a prototype of cloud mobile health monitoring system. The Computing Research Repository (2012)
3. Lustrek, M., Kaluza, B., Cvetkovic, B., Dovgan, E., Gjoreski, H., Mirchevska, V., Gams, M.: Confidence: ubiquitous care system to support independent living. DEMO at European Conference on Artificial Intelligence, pp. 1013–1014 (2012)
4. Abowd, G.D., Dey, A.K.: Towards a better understanding of context and context-awareness. In: Gellersen, H.-W. (ed.) HUC 1999. LNCS, vol. 1707, pp. 304–307. Springer, Heidelberg (1999)
5. Vyas, N., Farringdon, J., Andre, D., Stivoric, J.I.: Machine learning and sensor fusion for estimating continuous energy expenditure. In: Innovative Applications of Artificial Intelligence Conference, pp. 1613–1620 (2012)
6. Hall, M.J., Fingerhut, L., Heinen, M.: National Trend Data on Hospitalization of the Elderly for Injuries, 1979-2001. American Public Health Association, APHA (2004)
7. Tinetti, M.E., Williams, C.S.: Falls, Injuries Due to Falls, and the Risk of Admission to a Nursing Home. The New England Journal of Medicine 337, 1279–1284 (1997)
8. Wild, D., Nayak, U.S., Isaacs, B.: How dangerous are falls in old people at home? British Medical Journal (Clinical Research Edition) 282(6260), 266–268 (1981, 1982)
9. Gjoreski, H., Luštrek, M., Gams, M.: Accelerometer Placement for Posture Recognition and Fall Detection. In: The 7th International Conference on Intelligent Environments, pp. 47–54 (2011)
10. PAMSys-The physical activity monitoring system (2012), http://www.biosensics.com/pamsys.html

11. Sukthankar, G., Sycara, K.: A cost minimization approach to human behavior recognition. In: 4th International Conference on Autonomous Agents and Multi-Agents Systems, pp. 1067–1074 (2005)
12. Kwapisz, J.R., Weiss, G.M., Moore, S.A.: Activity recognition using cell phone accelerometers. ACM SIGKDD Explorer. 12, 74–82 (2010)
13. Wu, H., Lemaire, E.D., Baddour, N.: Activity change-of-state identification using a Blackberry smartphone. Journal of Medical and Biological Engineering 32, 265–272 (2012)
14. Lai, C., Huang, Y.M., Park, J.H., Chao, H.C.: Adaptive body posture analysis for elderly-falling detection with multisensors. IEEE Intelligent Systems 25, 2–11 (2010)
15. Gjoreski, H., Luštrek, M., Gams, M.: Context-Based Fall Detection using Inertial and Location Sensors. In: Paternò, F., de Ruyter, B., Markopoulos, P., Santoro, C., van Loenen, E., Luyten, K. (eds.) AmI 2012. LNCS, vol. 7683, pp. 1–16. Springer, Heidelberg (2012)
16. Ravi, N., Dandekar, N., Mysore, P., Littman, M.L.: Activity recognition from accelerometer data. In: 17th Conference on Innovative Applications of Artificial Intelligence, pp. 1541–1546 (2005)
17. Jantaraprim, P., Phukpattaranont, P., Limsakul, C., Wongkittisuksa, B.: Evaluation of Fall Detection for the Elderly on a Variety of Subject Groups. In: i-CREATe (2009)
18. Shan, S., Yuan, T.: A Wearable Pre-Impact Fall Detector Using Feature Selection and Support Vector Machine. In: 10th IEEE International Conference on Signal Processing, pp. 1686–1689 (2010)
19. Nguyen, T.-T., Cho, M.-C., Lee, T.-S.: Automatic Fall Detection Using Wearable Biomedical Signal Measurement Terminal. In: 31st Annual International Conference of the IEEE EMBS, pp. 5203–5206 (2009)
20. Zhang, T., Wang, J., Xu, L., Liu, P.: Fall Detection by Wearable Sensor and One-Class SVM Algorithm. In: Huang, D.-S., Li, K., Irwin, G.W. (eds.) ICIC 2006. LNCIS, vol. 345, pp. 858–863. Springer, Heidelberg (2006)
21. Shimmer sensor platform, http://www.shimmer-research.com
22. Tapia, E.M.: Using machine learning for real-time activity recognition and estimation of energy expenditure. Ph.D. Thesis, Massachusetts Institute of Technology (2008)
23. Kozina, S., Gjoreski, H., Gams, M., Lustrek, M.: Three-layer Activity Recognition Combining Domain Knowledge and Meta-classification. Journal of Medical and Biological Engineering, doi:10.5405/jmbe.1321
24. Weka application programming interface, API (2012), http://weka.sourceforge.net/doc

Multisensor Data Fusion for Activity Recognition Based on Reservoir Computing

Filippo Palumbo[1,2], Paolo Barsocchi[1], Claudio Gallicchio[2], Stefano Chessa[1,2], and Alessio Micheli[2]

[1] ISTI Institute of CNR, Pisa Research Area, via Moruzzi 1, I-56124, Pisa, Italy
{filippo.palumbo,paolo.barsocchi,stefano.chessa}@isti.cnr.it
[2] Computer Science Department, University of Pisa, Pisa, Italy
{palumbo,gallicch,ste,micheli}@di.unipi.it

Abstract. Ambient Assisted Living facilities provide assistance and care for the elderly, where it is useful to infer their daily activity for ensuring their safety and successful ageing. In this work, we present an Activity Recognition system that classifies a set of common daily activities exploiting both the data sampled by accelerometer sensors carried out by the user and the reciprocal Received Signal Strength (RSS) values coming from worn wireless sensor devices and from sensors deployed in the environment. To this end, we model the accelerometer and the RSS stream, obtained from a Wireless Sensor Network (WSN), using Recurrent Neural Networks implemented as efficient Echo State Networks (ESNs), within the Reservoir Computing paradigm. Our results show that, with an appropriate configuration of the ESN, the system reaches a good accuracy with a low deployment cost.

Keywords: AAL, Activity Recognition, Neural Networks, Sensor Data Fusion, WSN.

1 Introduction

Activity Recognition (AR) is an emerging field of research, that takes its motivations from established research fields such as ubiquitous computing, context-aware computing and multimedia. Recognizing everyday life activities is a challenging application in pervasive computing, with a lot of interesting developments in the health care domain, the human behavior modeling domain and the human-machine interaction domain [1]. From the point of view of the deployment of the activity recognition solutions, we recognize two main approaches depending on whether the solution adopts wearable devices or not. The solutions that make use of wearable devices are the more established and studied. In these solutions the wearable devices are generally sensors (for example embedding accelerometers, or transducers for physiological measures) that make direct measures about the user activities. For example, a sensor placed on the user ankle may detect the number of steps based on the response of an embedded accelerometer that is shaked with a specific pattern every time the user makes

J.A. Botía et al. (Eds.): EvAAL 2013, CCIS 386, pp. 24–35, 2013.
© Springer-Verlag Berlin Heidelberg 2013

a step. On the other hand, the disadvantage of this approach is that wearable devices can be intrusive on the user, even if, with recent advances in technologies of embedded systems, sensors tend to be smaller and smaller. Solutions that avoid the use of wearable devices instead, are motivated by the need for a less intrusive activity recognition systems. Among these solutions, those based on cameras are probably the most common [2]. However, even though this approach is physically less intrusive for the user, it suffers from several issues: low image resolution, target occlusion and time-consuming processing, which is still a challenge for real-time activity recognition systems. Furthermore, user privacy is also an important issue, especially if cameras are used to continuously monitor the user itself. More recently, a new generation of non wearable solution is emerging. These solution exploits the implicit alteration of the wireless channel due to the movements of the user, which is measured by devices placed in the environment and that measure the Received Signal Strength (RSS) of the beacon packets they exchange among themselves [3]. In our activity recognition system we use a mix of the two approaches. Specifically we use both wearable and environmental sensors and we base the recognition of the user activity both on accelerometers embedded on the wearable sensors and on the RSS of the beacon packets exchanged between all the sensors (both wearable and environmental). A second important achievement of our system is the use of a distributed machine learning approach, in which the sensors themselves perform activity classification by using embedded learning modules. Specifically, in the class of Recurrent Neural Network, we take into consideration the efficient Reservoir Computing (RC) [4] paradigm in general, and the Echo State Network (ESN) [5, 6] model in particular. In order to support distributed neural computation on the sensors we use a Learning Layer: a software component developed within the framework of the Rubicon project [7] that implements a distributed ESN embedded in the sensors and in more powerful devices such as PCs or gateways. We base our approach on some recent works [8–10] that classify activities based on accelerometer (in fact, accelerometers have been widely accepted due to their compact size, their low-power requirement, low cost, non-intrusiveness and capacity to provide data directly related to the motion of people) and on some of our recent works in which we used RSS and neural networks to make predictions on user movements [11–16]. To the best of our knowledge, this is the first work that investigates the use of common wireless sensor devices deployed in the environment in combination with wearable sensors embedding accelerometers, in order to increase the performance of the activity recognition system. The rest of the paper is organized as follows. Section 2 presents a reference scenario, Section 3 describes the overall architecture of the activity recognition system, and Section 4 anticipates some experimental results about the performance of our system. Finally, Section 5 draws the conclusions.

2 Scenario

The main objective of the proposed system is to implement an activity recognition system (ARS) that recognizes the following activities: Walking, standing up, sitting down, lying down, bending, falling and cycling (using a stationary bike). The main critical issues for the proposed system are due to the unknown environment (the CIAMI Living Lab in Valencia), and the unknown actor that will perform the activities during the competition. For this reason we plan to use a sensor network that is partly worn by the user and partly deployed in the environment. Specifically, we plan to use 5 wearable and 4 environmental sensors. The sensors are capable of measuring the signal strength of the incoming packets, and also embed a two axis accelerometer. The wearable sensors are placed on the chest, on the arms and on the ankles of the user. Each wearable sensor measures accelerometer values from its embedded two-axis accelerometer. Furthermore, the wearable sensors, which are connected in a clique, exchange among themselves beacon packets, with the purpose of measuring the respective RSS among themselves. All the data acquired by the wearable sensors are collected by the gateway that also runs a centralized instance of the Learning Layer to make predictions about all the activities of the user. The environmental sensors filters the beacon packets emitted by the wearable sensors to receive only to the beacons emitted by the sensor on the chest. Each of these environmental sensors embed the learning layer and make a prediction about the walking activity. The predictions of the environmental sensors are sent to the gateway that also implements a voting system to output the most likely activity of the user (Fig. 1).

3   Architecture of the Proposed Solution

The implementation of the system leverages on a number of sensors (some wearable and some other environmental) and a gateway that run the RUBICON Learning Layer (LL) developed in an ongoing European project [7]. The LL offers a distributed, general purpose learning system where independent learning modules are embedded on sensors and on the gateways. Such learning modules are capable of addressing a large variety of computational learning tasks through a scalable distributed architecture comprising independent RC learning modules deployed on a variety of devices, including sensors. Since the LL is still under development, due to the current software limitations it is not possible at the moment to process on the sensors all the tasks required to detect all the activities defined in the EvAAL benchmarks. For this reason our deployed solution leverages on the LL for the distributed detection of the walking activity, and reverts to a centralized processing on the gateway for the other activities. In perspective, as the RUBICON project will deliver new and more stable version of the software, our plan is to embed all the tasks for all the activities directly on the sensors. In this way the activity recognition will not require anymore the presence of a gateway (which, however, may still be necessary but only to provide the output of the activity recognition system to the user). The next subsections describe the data processing and integration, and briefly review the RUBICON Learning Layer.

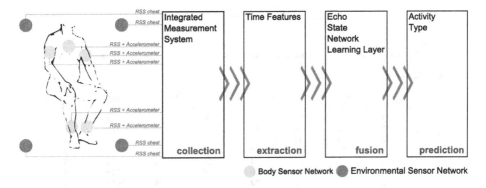

Fig. 1. Illustration of the RC-based multisensor data fusion algorithm

3.1 Sensor Data Processing and Integration

Depending on the tests that we will run before the actual competition, we will use either the TMote [17] or the Iris [18] platform. Anyway, both platforms embed a radio subsystem compatible with the IEEE 802.15.4 standard and they are both capable of measuring the signal strength of the incoming packets, and also embed a two axis accelerometers. As shown in Fig. 1 an integrated measurement system, placed on the gateway in the case of a centralized processing and on the sensor in the distributed detection of the walking activity, collects the payloads of the beacon packets, filters data discarding bad packets and taking into account possible packet losses, and send the filtered data to the features extraction module. For the purpose of communications, the beacon packets are exchanged by using a simple virtual token protocol that completes its execution in a time slot of 0.1 seconds. As a result, each wearable sensor produces every 0.1 seconds a vector of 4 RSS values from the other sensors and its X and Y accelerometer values (Fig. 2). The environmental sensors will produce only RSS values between themselves and the wearable sensor placed on the chest. Fig. 2 shows in the Sensed Values section the raw data exchanged between the sensor nodes. Instead of directly using raw sensor data that contain redundant information as input for the ESN data fusion algorithm, time-domain features were first extracted to train the fusion model and determine model parameters. In this study, 40 features were extracted from the wearable sensors for every 200 ms data segment step time, corresponding to 2 time slot used by the virtual token protocol. The step time is a configurable parameter in our system that lets us collect more values to use in the feature extraction module when we want to. The time-domain features, shown in the Aggregate Values section of Fig. 2, included the mean value and standard deviation for each reciprocal RSS reading and accelerometer on the x and y axis. Based on these features the ESN Learning Layer and the voting system make a prediction about the activity type of the user.

```
                              ┌─────────────┐
──────────────────────────────┤ Sample Data ├────────────────────────────
                              └─────────────┘
Source
-------
      No. Sensors: 5        Time Slot [ms]: 100      Step Time [ms]: 200

Sensed Values
-------------
      Sensor i   RSSi1   RSSi2   RSSi3   RSSi4   RSSi5   ACCiX   ACCiY
      ------------------------------------------------------------------
           1       0      24      18      25      27      534     449
           2      23       0      31      18      24      481     441
           3      16      31       0      27      23      494     458
           4      26      18      27       0      52      500     422
           5      26      24      24      51       0      514     465
           1       0      24      20      26      25      532     448
           2      23       0      32      17      24      482     441
           3      18      31       0      27      23      493     457
           4      26      18      27       0      52      499     422
           5      24      24      22      51       0      514     464

Aggregate Values
----------------
      Timestamp 1368548213503

         M12    M13    M14    M15    M23    M24    M25    M34    M35    M45
        23.50  18.00  25.75  25.50  31.25  17.75  24.00  27.00  23.00  51.50

         SD12   SD13   SD14   SD15   SD23   SD24   SD25   SD34   SD35   SD45
         0.50   1.41   0.43   1.12   0.43   0.43   0.00   0.00   0.71   0.50

         M1X    M1Y    M2X    M2Y    M3X    M3Y    M4X    M4Y    M5X    M5Y
        533.00 448.50 481.50 441.00 493.50 457.50 499.50 422.00 514.00 464.50

         SD1X   SD1Y   SD2X   SD2Y   SD3X   SD3Y   SD4X   SD4Y   SD5X   SD5Y
         1.00   0.50   0.50   0.00   0.50   0.50   0.50   0.00   0.00   0.50
```

Fig. 2. A sample data segment with Source, Sensed Values, and Aggregate Values for a Step Time of 200 ms

3.2 RUBICON Learning Layer

The RUBICON Learning Layer (LL) implement a distributed, general purpose learning system where independent learning modules are embedded on sensors and on more powerful devices, e.g. gateways or PCs. The high-level goal of LL is to deliver short-term predictions based on the temporal history of the input signals. This can be easily applied to the recognition of human activities. The software of the LL is organized into 3 subsystems:

- The Learning Network (LN) (Fig. 3(a)) that implements an adaptive environmental memory by means of a distributed learning components. The LN components hosted on the sensors are implemented in TinyOS [19], while the LN components hosted on PCs or gateways are implemented in Java. The LN modules (represented in Fig. 3(a)) reside on devices (either sensors, PCs or gateways) with heterogeneous computational capabilities. The distributed LN components cooperate through Synaptic Connections (thin arrows in Fig. 3(a)) to perform a distributed neural computation. Each individual module may processes local information obtained from the embedded transducers (if they are available) and remote inputs received from other learning modules (such remote inputs are delivered through the Synaptic Connection mechanism). As a whole, the LN subsystem, implements the assigned computational learning tasks by providing the run-time predictions. Furthermore, the LN supports online refining the learned tasks by using on teaching signals that may be provided by the user.

– The Learning Network Manager (LNM) that is a Java software agent hosted on a gateway, that is responsible for the setup and management of the LL. The Learning Network Manager (LNM) manages the learning phase and the configuration of the LN. To this purpose it instructs the LN to set up or destroy Synaptic Connections, to dynamically attach a learning module to the LN when a new sensor joins the network, or to recover from the failure (or disconnection) of a learning module by reassigning the tasks previously run by that module to other available devices.

– The Training Manager (TN) (Fig. 3(b)) a Java software agent hosted on a gateway that is responsible for the learning phases of the LL and for the management, training and self-adaptation of the LN. It comprises the Training Agent, the Network Mirror and a Repository. The Training Agent manages the activation of the training phases of the LL by processing the control instructions received from the LNM and by orchestrating the learning in the Network Mirror component through appropriate control messages, it receives online learning feedbacks from the user, and administers the appropriate refinement signals to the LN, and it receives training data and stores them in the Repository (training data are used for the incremental training on novel computational tasks that, once appropriately learned, can be deployed to the LN. The Network Mirror comprises a data structure that contains a mirror of each of the components of the LN. This allows a centralized the retraining of the LN, since a retraining on low power devices such as the sensors is not feasible). The mirrored copies of the LN components are also used to support the recovery from the loss of a device: if a LN components disappears because the hosting device fails (or gets disconnected) a new LN component on another device can be instructed to take over the disappeared tasks by using the mirrored copy of the lost LN component.

In its current design, the LL is suitable to address tasks that can be modeled as time-series prediction problems. For example, these tasks include event detection, localization and movement prediction using signal strength information, and basic human activities recognition.

3.3   ESN

An ESN ([5, 6])is composed of an input layer with N_U unit, a reservoir layer with N_R units and a readout layer with N_Y units. The typical architecture of an ESN is shown in Figure 4. The reservoir is a large layer of sparsely connected nonlinear recurrent units, used to encode the input history of the driving input signal

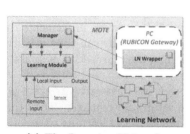

(a) The Learning Network.   (b) The Training Manager.

Fig. 3. The RUBICON Learning Layer

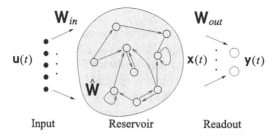

Input   Reservoir   Readout

Fig. 4. Architecture of an ESN with $N_U = 5$ input units, $N_R = 9$ reservoir units and $N_Y = 2$ readout units

into a finite dimensional state. The readout is an output layer of linear feed-forward units, and represents the only trained part of the network architecture. At each time step t, the reservoir of the LI-ESN computes the state $\mathbf{x}(t) \in \mathbb{R}^{N_R}$ according to the state transition function

$$\mathbf{x}(t) = \tanh(\mathbf{W}_{in}\mathbf{u}(t) + \hat{\mathbf{W}}\mathbf{x}(t-1)) \tag{1}$$

where $\mathbf{u}(t) \in \mathbb{R}^{N_U}$ is the input for the ESN at pass t, $\mathbf{W}_{in} \in \mathbb{R}^{N_R} \times N_U$ is the input-to-reservoir weight matrix (possibly including a bias term), $\hat{\mathbf{W}} \in \mathbb{R}^{N_R \times N_R}$ is the reservoir recurrent weight matrix. The output of the network at pass t, i.e. $\mathbf{y}(t) \in \mathbb{R}^{N_Y}$, is computed by the readout part of the ESN, as a linear combination of the reservoir units activation:

$$\mathbf{y}(t) = \mathbf{W}_{out}\mathbf{x}(t) \tag{2}$$

where $\mathbf{W}_{out} \in \mathbb{R}^{N_Y \times N_R}$ is the reservoir-to-readout weight matrix. Reservoir parameters are left untrained after random initialization under the constraints given by the Echo State Property (ESP) [5, 6]. The ESP essentially states that the reservoir state dynamics asymptotically depends only on the history of the input signals, and dependencies on the initial state conditions are progressively lost. A sufficient and a necessary conditions are known in literature for the ESP to be satisfied. For practical applications the sufficient condition is often considered too restrictive, and the following necessary condition is typically used:

$$\rho(\hat{\mathbf{W}}) < 1 \tag{3}$$

where $\rho(\hat{\mathbf{W}})$ is the spectral radius of the matrix $\hat{\mathbf{W}}$. Accordingly, the reservoir weight matrix $\mathbf{W}$ is randomly initialized and then re-scaled such that the condition in equation 3 holds. The weight values in matrix $\mathbf{W}_{in}$ are randomly chosen from a uniform distribution over $[-scale_{in}, scale_{in}]$, where $scale_{in}$ is an input scaling parameter. The weight values in matrix $\mathbf{W}_{out}$ are the only one subject to training, usually by using efficient linear methods such as Moore-Penrose pseudo-inversion and ridge regression (see e.g. [4]). The RC approach, and the ESN model in particular, have been recently successfully applied to real-world problems in the field of AAL. The experiments presented in [11–14] have indeed shown that RC modules achieve extremely good predictive performances in AAL tasks, being able to generalize the predictions to unseen environments [11, 14]. The study of the relation between the predictive performance and the cost of the system deployment on the one hand, and the computational cost of the ESN (in terms of memory and time) on the other hand, pointed out the feasibility of the RC approach in this context [11, 12]. By adopting suitable strategies for the encoding of the network weights, it has been shown that a memory occupation below 2 Kb or RAM is sufficient to obtain good accuracy results [11], opening the way for practical embedding of the ESNs on the motes of a WSN for AAL applications, within the scopes of the RUBICON project.

4   Experimental Results

Recognizing human activities depends directly on the features extracted for motion analysis. In this test we use a sensor network, worn by the user, that is able to provide two separated accelerometer data time series, one time series for acceleration on each axis Ax and Ay, and the RSS among each sensor of the network. The accelerometer data together with the reciprocal RSS time series are then combined by using neural computation to provide future forecasts based on previous measurements. As a proof of concepts two out of seven activities will be tested in laboratory: standing up and sitting down.

4.1   Setup

In these tests the sensor network is composed of five IRIS nodes embedding a Chipcon AT86RF230 radio subsystem that implements the IEEE 802.15.4 standard (Figure 5). Five sensors, in the following Body Sensor Network (BSN), are placed on the user (on each arm and on each ankle and one on the chest), while a sink, always in line of sight with the BSN, collects the accelerometer

Fig. 5. The wireless sensor devices used to collect both accelerometer and RSS data

data together with the reciprocal RSS. The x-axis of the worn accelerometers pointed out along subject's sagittal plane and its y-axis pointed down along his coronal plane.

4.2   Data and Results

Test subject was asked to perform the group of activities 25 times. Sitting down and standing up are very short time activities, so only 12 sample data for each test were collected. Fig. 6 shows sample RSS data between sensor 3 and 4, between sensor 3 and 5, and sensor 3 accelerometer data for each test activity. Sensor 3 is the one placed on the chest while 4 and 5 are the sensors placed at the right and left ankles, respectively. As we can see from Fig. 6 when the subject sits down the RSS signal quickly increases in its value, then slightly decreases and finally assess to an higher value than the initial one. This pattern is due to the typical vertical momentum pattern of the sitting down activity [20, 21]. Similarly, when the subject stands up, a first movement of the chest toward the ankles is done, then it turns away and finally stand up reporting a final rss value lower than the corresponding value for initial sitting position. Also the y-axis component of the accelerometer placed on the chest shows values very indicative of the direction of movement. The collection of all sample data from all sensors together with their accelerometer data was used for the definition of a benchmark dataset for activity recognition, comprising a total number of 50 input sequences. A classification task was thereby constructed by assigning a target output value, i.e. -1 for the activity of sitting and $+1$ for the activity of standing. In our experiments we used ESNs adopting an hyper-parametrization setting inspired from our previous experimental investigations on RC applications to AAL tasks [11–14]. Specifically, we used reservoir with $N_R = 50$ units, spectral radius $\rho(\hat{\mathbf{W}}) = 0.99$, input scaling parameter $scale_{in} = 0.01$. Readouts were trained using ridge regression, with regularization parameter $\lambda_r = 0.01$. The benchmark dataset described above was split in a training set and a test set containing 32 and 18 samples, respectively. A number of 10 reservoir guesses were considered, and the results were averaged over such guesses. The accuracy

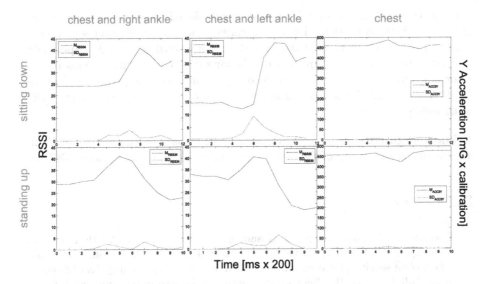

Fig. 6. Sample benchmark dataset for activity recognition. Each row shows mean and standard deviation of RSSI and accelerometer data of a single sample for each test activity. Sitting down and standing up respectively. First column shows RSSI values between sensor 3 and 4. Second column shows RSSI values between sensor 3 and 5. Third column shows the chest sensor accelerometer data.

achieved by the ESN modules was 100% in training and 91.11% in test. Such good results, in line with those obtained in our previous works [11–16], represent a clear indication of the effectiveness of our proposed approach for the activity recognition tasks of the type considered.

5   Conclusions

In this work, we present an activity recognition system that classifies activities exploiting both the data sampled by accelerometer sensors carried out by the user and the RSS values coming from worn wireless sensor devices and from sensors deployed in the environment. The proposed activity recognition system uses a mix of two approaches, i.e. wearable and not wearable. Specifically, we use both wearable and environmental sensors and we base the recognition of the user activity both on accelerometers embedded on the wearable sensors and on the RSS of the beacon packets exchanged between all the sensors (both wearable and environmental). The accelerometer and the RSS stream thus obtained are modelled by using Recurrent Neural Networks implemented as efficient Echo State Networks (ESNs), within the Reservoir Computing paradigm. In particular, the proposed system is able to use a distributed machine learning approach, in which the sensors themselves perform activity classification by using embedded learning modules. Since the Learning Layer (LL) module is still under development, due to the current software limitations it is not possible at the moment to process on the sensors all the tasks required to detect all the activities defined in the EvAAL benchmarks. For this reason our deployed solution leverages on the LL for the distributed detection of the walking activity, and reverts to a centralized processing on the gateway for the other activities. In this paper only two out of seven activities are tested achieving 91.1% of accuracy. This result, according with the results obtained in our previous works, represent a clear indication of the effectiveness of our approach also when all the seven activity will be considered.

Acknowledgments. This work was supported in part by the European Commission in the framework of the FP7 project universAAL under Contract 247950.

References

1. Choudhury, T., LaMarca, A., LeGrand, L., Rahimi, A., Rea, A., Borriello, G., Hemingway, B., Koscher, K., Lan, J.A., Lester, J., Wyatt, D., Haehnel, D., et al.: The mobile sensing platform: An embedded activity recognition system (2008)
2. Khawandi, S., Daya, B., Chauvet, P.: Automated monitoring system for fall detection in the elderly. International Journal of Image Processing 4(5) (2010)
3. Bocca, M., Kaltiokallio, O., Patwari, N.: Radio tomographic imaging for ambient assisted living. In: Chessa, S., Knauth, S. (eds.) EvAAL 2012. CCIS, vol. 362, pp. 108–130. Springer, Heidelberg (2013)
4. Lukosevicius, M., Jaeger, H.: Reservoir computing approaches to recurrent neural network training. Computer Science Review 3(3), 127–149 (2009)
5. Jaeger, H., Haas, H.: Harnessing nonlinearity: Predicting chaotic systems and saving energy in wireless communication. Science 304(5667), 78–80 (2004)
6. Jaeger, H.: The "echo state" approach to analysing and training recurrent neural networks. Technical report, GMD (2001)
7. Bacciu, D., Gallicchio, C., Lenzi, A., Chessa, S., Micheli, A., Pelagatti, S., Vairo, C.: Distributed neural computation over WSN in ambient intelligence. In: van Berlo, A., Hallenborg, K., Rodríguez, J.M.C., Tapia, D.I., Novais, P. (eds.) Ambient Intelligence – Software & Applications. AISC, vol. 219, pp. 147–154. Springer, Heidelberg (2013)
8. Ravi, N., Dandekar, N., Mysore, P., Littman, M.L.: Activity recognition from accelerometer data. In: Proceedings of the Seventeenth Conference on Innovative Applications of Artificial Intelligence (IAAI), pp. 1541–1546. AAAI Press (2005)
9. Bao, L., Intille, S.S.: Activity recognition from user-annotated acceleration data. In: Ferscha, A., Mattern, F. (eds.) PERVASIVE 2004. LNCS, vol. 3001, pp. 1–17. Springer, Heidelberg (2004)
10. Mannini, A., Sabatini, A.M.: Machine learning methods for classifying human physical activity from on-body accelerometers. Sensors 10(2), 1154–1175 (2010)
11. Bacciu, D., Barsocchi, P., Chessa, S., Gallicchio, C., Micheli, A.: An experimental characterization of reservoir computing in ambient assisted living applications. Neural Computing and Applications, 1–14 (2013)
12. Bacciu, D., Chessa, S., Gallicchio, C., Micheli, A., Barsocchi, P.: An experimental evaluation of reservoir computation for ambient assisted living. In: Apolloni, B., Bassis, S., Esposito, A., Morabito, F.C. (eds.) Neural Nets and Surroundings. SIST, vol. 19, pp. 41–50. Springer, Heidelberg (2013)

13. Gallicchio, C., Micheli, A., Barsocchi, P., Chessa, S.: User movements forecasting by reservoir computing using signal streams produced by mote-class sensors. In: Ser, J., Jorswieck, E., Miguez, J., Matinmikko, M., Palomar, D., Salcedo-Sanz, S., Gil-Lopez, S. (eds.) MOBILIGHT 2011. LNICST, vol. 81, pp. 151–168. Springer, Heidelberg (2012)
14. Bacciu, D., Gallicchio, C., Micheli, A., Barsocchi, P., Chessa, S.: Predicting user movements in heterogeneous indoor environments by reservoir computing. In: Proceedings of the 22nd International Joint Conference on Artificial Intelligence (IJCAI 2011), Space, Time and Ambient Intelligence Workshop (STAMI 2011), July 16-22, pp. 1–8 (2011)
15. Guraliuc, A., Barsocchi, P., Potort, F., Nepa, P.: Limb movements classification using wearable wireless transceivers. IEEE Transactions on Information Technology in Biomedicine 15(3), 474–480 (2011)
16. Barsocchi, P.: Position recognition to support bedsores prevention. IEEE Journal of Biomedical and Health Informatics 17(1), 53–59 (2013)
17. TelosB: Tmote sky, http://www.capsil.org/capsilwiki/index.php/TELOSB/TMote_Sky (accessed: May 18, 2013)
18. Moog: Crossbow, http://www.xbow.com (accessed: May 18, 2013)
19. TinyOS: Tinyos, http://www.tinyos.net/ (accessed: May 18, 2013)
20. Ashford, S., De Souza, L.: A comparison of the timing of muscle activity during sitting down compared to standing up. Physiotherapy Research International 5(2), 111–128 (2000)
21. Kralj, A., Jaeger, R.J., Munih, M.: Analysis of standing up and sitting down in humans: definitions and normative data presentation. Journal of Biomechanics 23(11), 1123–1138 (1990)

Activity Recognition System Using Non-intrusive Devices through a Complementary Technique Based on Discrete Methods

Miguel Ángel Álvarez de la Concepción[1], Luis Miguel Soria Morillo[1],
Luis González Abril[2], and Juan Antonio Ortega Ramírez[1]

[1] Computer Languages and Systems Dept., University of Seville, 41012 Seville, Spain
{maalvarez,lsoria,jortega}@us.es
[2] Applied Economics I Dept., University of Seville, 41018 Seville, Spain
luisgon@us.es

Abstract. This paper aims to develop a cheap, comfortable and, specially, efficient system which controls the physical activity carried out by the user. For this purpose an extended approach to physical activity recognition is presented, based on the use of discrete variables which employ data from accelerometer sensors. To this end, an innovative selection, discretization and classification technique to make the recognition process in an efficient way and at low energy cost, is presented in this work based on Ameva discretization. Entire process is executed on the smartphone and on a wireless health monitoring system is used when the smartphone is not used taking into account the system energy consumption.

Keywords: Contextual Information, Discretization Method, Mobile Environment, Qualitative Systems, Smart-Energy Computing.

1 Introduction

In recent years, thanks largely to the increased interest on monitoring certain sectors of population such as elderly people with dementia or people in rehabilitation, activity recognition systems have experienced an increase in both number and quality results. However, most of them are in a high computational cost and hence, it cannot be executed into a general purpose mobile device.

Calculation of the physical activity of a user based on data obtained from an accelerometer is a current research topic. Furthermore, many works is going to be analyzed showing some identified limitations that make these systems uncomfortable for users in general.

The first difference observed between the systems developed is the type of used sensor. There are systems using specific hardware [1], while others use general purpose hardware [2]. Obviously, the use of generic hardware is a benefit for users, since the cost of devices and versatility of them are points in their favor. Not to mention decreasing the loss and forgetting risk due to they have been integrated on an everyday object like users' smartphones.

J.A. Botía et al. (Eds.): EvAAL 2013, CCIS 386, pp. 36–47, 2013.

Another difference found between the surveyed proposals is the number and position of the sensors. In [3] can be seen that the accelerometer sensor is placed in a glove and a multitude of activities depending on the movement of the hand are recognized. In contrast, other studies use various sensors throughout the body [4], [5] or a wearable wireless sensor node with a static wireless non-intrusive sensory infrastructure [6] to recognize these activities. According to some comparative studies and previous works based on multiple sensors, they are more accurate.

Although, works like [2], where a sensor is at users' pocket or in the hipe, is more comfortable for them. By this way, place them in the monitored person is easier, not to mention that the infrastructure is much lower.

Thus, the presented work will is focus on the recognition of physical activities carried out by users throughout their mobile devices. So, it must be paid special attention to energy consumption and computational cost of used methods. Also, a wireless health monitoring system can be used to increment the user acceptance, i.e. the user does not carry the mobile devices all the time in an indoor environment.

One step further, some works do not only use data from accelerometers, but use other sources such as microphone, light sensor or voice recognition to determine the context of the user [7]. However, they present problems i.e. when the environment is noisy or the user is alone.

There are related works where data for activities recognition are obtained through mobile devices, but these data are sent to a server to process the information [8]. Thus, computational cost is not a handicap and because of this more complex methods are used. In contrast, the efficiency is a crucial issue when processing is carried out in the mobile device [9], [10].

To reduce the cost associated to accelerometer signal analysis, this paper opts for a novel approach based on a discretization method. Thanks to discretization process, classification cost is much lower than working with continuous variables. Because of this, it is possible to eliminate the correlation between variables during the recognition process and on the other hand, to minimize the energy consumption from the process.

Working in the domain of discrete variables to perform learning and recognition of activities is a new approach offered by this work. This decision was largely due to the high computational cost required for learning algorithms based on continuous variables used for this purpose over the years.

In [11], a labeling process, like a discretization process, is used to obtain a Qualitative Similarity Index (QSI), so it can be said that a transformation of the continuous domain to the discrete domain of values of the variables is beneficial in certain aspects.

But, before the self-recognition or learning, it is necessary to carry out a process of Ameva discretization from its algorithm [12]. It has a number of advantages over other well-known discretization algorithms like CAIM discretization algorithm [13], i.e. it is unsupervised and very fast. The most notable of these is the small number of intervals generated which facilitates and reduces the computational cost of the recognition process.

It should be noted that many of these studies could be seen in action during the competition EvAAL 2012 [14] in Activity recognition track. EvAAL is an annual international competition that addresses the challenge of evaluation and comparison of Ambient Assisted Living (AAL) systems and platforms, with the final goal to assess the autonomy, independent living and quality of life that AAL systems may grant to their end users.

In this track competition, four teams participated in the challenge: CUJ (from the University of Chiba, Japan) [15], CMU (from Carnegie Mellon and Utah Universities, USA) [16], DCU (from Dublin City University, Ireland) [17] and USS (from University of Seville, Spain) [12]. Finally, although CMU had the best accuracy in the results, USS won the competition because its simplicity and interoperability gave good marks in all the evaluated criteria.

In order to improve the accuracy problems encountered during the celebration of the EvAAL 2012 competition, some significant improvements in Ameva discretization algorithm are proposed. Also, in addition to detect specific activities, the barometric sensor which is being included in the latest generation of mobile devices is used.

Finally, in order to answer the question about what would happen if you decide not to use your mobile device in an indoor environment, as happens in real life, a complementary wireless device is also optionally used.

There are other similar EvAAL competitions such as HARL [18], OPPORTUNITY [19], HASC [20] or BSN contest [21].

The paper is organized as follows: first, the activity recognition step is presented in Section 2. Also, the data collection and the set of activities are presented. Section 3 presents the methodology to determine the activity using the Ameva discretization. Section 4 reports the obtained results of applying the methodology. Finally, the paper conclusions with a summary of the most important points are in Section 5.

2   Activity Recognition

The final real system consist only of a smartphone and, optionally, a wireless device, configured to detect the competition activities: lie, sit, stand, walk, bend, fall and cycle.

2.1   Data Collection

In contrast to the needs of some studies that require a training set to classify a recognized activity correctly, this paper reduces the waiting time for recognition, providing valid information for an activity frequently.

To this end, a training set and a recognition set are obtained using 5-second-time windows of fixed duration which has been determined empirically as optimum length from a performance and an accuracy analysis of the system.

The time length of five seconds of these windows has been chosen because for our system is very important to ensure that in each time window there is at least one cycle of activity, where activity cycle is defined as a complete execution of some activity patterns. For example, two steps are a walking activity cycle and one pedal stroke is the activity cycle for cycling. If at least one cycle of activity can not be guaranteed in each time window, it is not possible to determine the activity from accelerometer patterns.

This analysis is performed based on the values obtained from the accelerometer, which significantly improve the precision of the body-related activities, and a barometer to detect environment-related activities, such as going upstairs and downstairs. The latter sensor has most often been integrated in recent mobile devices, allow to increase the overall system accuracy detection of activities.

So, based on these time windows that contain data for each accelerometer axis and reducing the computational cost of the new solution, signal module has been chosen to work. This eliminates the problem caused by the device rotation [22]. Furthermore, it increases user comfort with the system by removing the restriction to keep the orientation during the learning and recognition process.

For each data in a time window size N, $a_i = (a_i^x, a_i^y, a_i^z)$, $i = 1, 2, \ldots, N$ where x, y and z represent the three accelerometer axis, the accelerometer module is defined as follow:

$$|a_i| = \sqrt{(a_i^x)^2 + (a_i^y)^2 + (a_i^z)^2}$$

Hence, the arithmetic mean, the minimum, the maximum, the median, the standard and the mean deviation, and the signal magnitude area statistics are obtained for each time window.

In addition to the above variables, hereafter called temporary variables, a new set of statistics called frequency-domain features from the frequency domain of the problem are generated. Thus, in order to obtain the frequency-domain features, Fast Fourier Transform (FFT) is applied for each time window.

For the barometer sensor, two measures are obtained for each time window: at the beginning and at the end, taking into account the difference between them.

$$b = b_N - b_1$$

It is important to note that in this case, the absolute value is not taken into account, contrary to what was done with the values obtained from the accelerometer.

2.2   Set of Activities

Far from being a static system, the number and type of activities recognized by the system depends on the user. Thanks to this proposal when users is carrying out activities that have not been learned before can be determined. This is achieved basing on the analysis of probability associated to each pattern while user is performing the activities. Obviously, the number of activities to be detected will impact on the accuracy of the system. Especially if acceleration patterns between activities are very similar.

For a large numbers of users could be interesting recognize a few activities, such as walking, sitting and falling. But for another users, activities like driving or biking would be important. However, to carry out a comparative analysis of the accuracy and performance of the discrete recognition method proposed below, 8 activities were taken into account. These activities are immobile, walking, running, jumping, cycling, drive, walking-upstairs and walking-downstairs.

Therefore, the learning system allows the user to decide what activities he/she wants the system to recognize. This is highly useful when the determination of certain very specific activities on monitored users is required.

3   Methodology

3.1   Ameva Algorithm

Let $X = \{x_1, x_2, \ldots, x_n\}$ be a data set of an attribute $\mathcal{X}$ of mixed-mode data such that each example x_i belongs to only one of the ℓ classes of class variable denoted by

$$C = \{C_1, C_2, \ldots, C_\ell\}, \ell \geq 2$$

A continuous attribute discretization is a function $\mathcal{D} : \mathcal{X} \to C$ which assigns a class $C_i \in C$ to each value $x \in X$ in the domain of property that is being discretized. Let us consider a discretization $\mathcal{D}$ which discretizes $\mathcal{X}$ into k discrete intervals:

$$\mathcal{L}(k; \mathcal{X}; C) = \{L_1, L_2, \ldots, L_k\}$$

where L_1 is the interval $[d_0, d_1]$ and L_j is the interval $(d_{j-1}, d_j]$, $j = 2, 3, \ldots, k$. Thus, a discretization variable is defined as $\mathcal{L}(k) = \mathcal{L}(k; \mathcal{X}; C)$ which verifies that, for all $x_i \in X$, a unique L_j exists such $x_i \in L_j$ that for $i = 1, 2, \ldots, n$ and $j = 1, 2, \ldots, k$. The discretization variable $\mathcal{L}(k)$ of $\mathcal{X}$ and the class variable C are treated from a descriptive point of view.

The main aim of the Ameva method [12] is to maximize the dependency relationship between the class labels C and the continuous-values attribute $\mathcal{L}(k)$, and at the same time to minimize the number of discrete intervals k. For this, the following statistic is used:

$$Ameva(k) = \frac{\chi^2(k)}{k(\ell - 1)} \; where \; \chi^2(k) = N \left(-1 + \sum_{i=1}^{\ell} \sum_{j=1}^{k} \frac{n_{ij}^2}{n_{i \cdot} n_{\cdot j}} \right)$$

and n_{ij} denotes the total number of continuous values belonging to the C_i class that are within the interval L_j, $n_{i \cdot}$ is the total number of instances belonging to the class C_i and $n_{\cdot j}$ is the total number of instances that belong to the interval L_j, for $i = 1, 2, \ldots, \ell$ and $j = 1, 2, \ldots, k$, fulfilling the following:

$$n_{i \cdot} = \sum_{j=1}^{k} n_{ij}, \quad n_{\cdot j} = \sum_{i=1}^{\ell} n_{ij}, \quad N = \sum_{i=1}^{\ell} \sum_{j=1}^{k} n_{ij}$$

The original developed algorithm to obtain the best intervals with the Ameva discretization is based on finding the cutoff points that provide the best coefficient. To do this, the values of the variables are sorted to find the first cut (local maximum). Then, it returns the next cut, and so on, until the Ameva coefficient does not improve. This behavior causes the complexity of the algorithm is quadratic order, $O(n^2)$. A graphic with three local maximums can be seen in Figure 1.

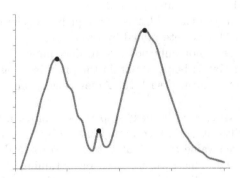

Fig. 1. An example of Ameva coefficient values with three local maximums

The presented improvement in this work allows to find all cuts, allowing the complexity of the algorithm would be of linear order, $O(n)$. Although there is a loss of precision, it is negligible for the field of study of this work, since it allows to obtain good results.

Finally, for each statistical $S_p \in \{S_1, S_2, \ldots, S_m\}$, the discretization process is performed, obtaining a matrix of order $k_p \times 2$, where k_p is the number of class intervals and 2 denotes the $inf(L_i^p)$ and $sup(L_i^p)$ interval limits i of p statistical. Hence, a three-dimensional matrix containing the statistics and the set of interval limits for each statistic is called Discretization Matrix and it is denoted by

$$\mathcal{W} = (w_{pij})$$

where $p = 1, 2, \ldots, m$, $i = 1, 2, \ldots, k_p$ and $j = 1, 2$.

Therefore, Discretization Matrix determines the interval at which each data belongs to the different statistical associated values, carrying out a simple and fast discretization process.

Class Integration. The aim in the next step of the algorithm is to provide a probability associated with the statistical data for each of the activities based on previously generated intervals. For this purpose, the elements of the training set $x \in X$ are processed to associate the label of the concrete activity in the training set. In addition, the value of each statistic is calculated based on the time window.

For carrying out the previous process, a Class Matrix, $\mathcal{V}$, is defined as a three-dimensional matrix that contains the number of data from the training set associated with a $\mathcal{L}$ interval in a $\mathcal{C}$ activity for each statistical $\mathcal{S}$ of the system. This matrix is defined as follows:

$$\mathcal{V} = (v_{pij})$$

where $v_{pij} = \#\{x \in X \mid inf(L_i^p) < x \leq sup(L_i^p)\}$, and $\mathcal{S} = S_p$, $\mathcal{C} = C_j$, $p = 1, 2, \ldots, m$, $i = 1, 2, \ldots, k_p$ and $j = 1, 2, \ldots, \ell$.

So, each position in the Class Matrix is uniquely associated with a position in the Discretization Matrix determined by its range.

At this point, there is not only possible to determine the discretization interval, but the Class Matrix helps to obtain the probability associated with the discretization process performed with the Ameva algorithm.

Activity-interval Matrix. The next step is determined a three-dimensional matrix, called Activity-Interval Matrix and denoted by $\mathcal{U}$, which determines the likelihood that a given value x associated to a S statistical corresponds to C activity in a $\mathcal{L}$ interval. This ratio is based on obtaining the goodness of the Ameva discretization and the aim is to determine the most probable activity from the data and the intervals generated for the training set.

Each value of $\mathcal{U}$ is defined as follows:

$$u_{pij} = \frac{v_{pij}}{v_{p \cdot j}} \frac{\sum_{q=1, q \neq j}^{\ell} \left(1 - \frac{v_{piq}}{v_{p \cdot q}}\right)}{\ell - 1} .$$

where $v_{p \cdot j}$ is the total number of time windows of the training process labeled with the j activity for the p statistic, and $p = 1, 2, \ldots, m$, $i = 1, 2, \ldots, k_p$ and $j = 1, 2, \ldots, \ell$

Given these values, $\mathcal{U}$ for the p statistic is defined as

$$\mathcal{U}_p = \begin{pmatrix} u_{p00} & \cdots & u_{p0j} & \cdots & u_{p0\ell} \\ \vdots & \ddots & \vdots & \ddots & \vdots \\ u_{pi0} & \cdots & u_{pij} & \cdots & u_{pi\ell} \\ \vdots & \ddots & \vdots & \ddots & \vdots \\ u_{pk_p0} & \cdots & u_{pk_pj} & \cdots & u_{pk_p\ell} \end{pmatrix}$$

As can be seen in the definition of $\mathcal{U}$, the likelihood that a data x is associated with the interval L_i corresponding to the activity C_j, depends not only on data, but all the elements associated with the interval L_i for the other activities.

Thus, each u_{pij} matrix position can be seen as a grade of belonging that a given x is identified to C_j activity, that it is included in the L_i interval of the S_p statistic.

Similarly, the elements of $\mathcal{U}$ have the following properties:

- $u_{pij} = 0 \iff v_{pij} = 0 \lor v_{piq} = v_{p \cdot q}, q \neq j$
- $u_{pij} = 1 \iff v_{pij} = v_{p \cdot j} = v_{pi}.$

Figure 2 shows the overall process described on this section for carry on data analysis and interval determination.

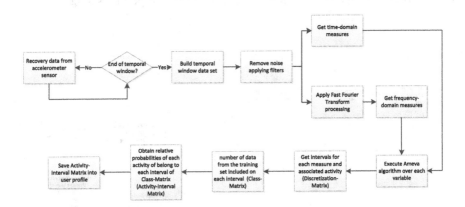

Fig. 2. Overall process of data analysis and interval determination

3.2   Classification Process

Having obtained the discretization intervals and the probabilities of belonging to each interval, the process by which the classification is performed can be described. This classification is based on data from the analysis of time windows. The process is divided into two main steps: the way in which to perform the recognition of physical activity is first described; and the process to determine the frequency at which some particular activity is then presented.

Classifying Data. For the classification process, the more likely activity is decided by a majority voting system. As said above, this process parts from the Activity-Interval Matrix and a set of data $x \in X$ for the $\mathcal{S}$ set.

Therefore, it consists in finding an activity $C_i \in C$ that maximizes the likelihood. The above criterion is collected in the following expression, denoted by mpa (most likely activity):

$$mpa(x) = C_k$$

where $k = arg(\max_j \sum_{p=1}^{m} u_{pij} \mid x \in (inf(L_i^p), sup(L_i^p)])$. The expression shows that the weight contributed by each statistical to the likely calculation function is the same. This can be done under the assumption that all statistical provide the same information to the system and there is not correlation between them.

Thus, the *mpa* represents the activity whose data, obtained through the processing time window, is more suited to the value set from $\mathcal{U}$. In this way, the proposed algorithm not only determine the *mpa*, but its associated probability.

From this likelihood, certain activities that do not adapt well to sets of generic classification can be identified. It is an indication that user is carrying out new activities for which the system has not been trained previously.

Figure 3 shows the overall process described on this section for recognition process from Activity-Interval Matrix calculated in the previous stage.

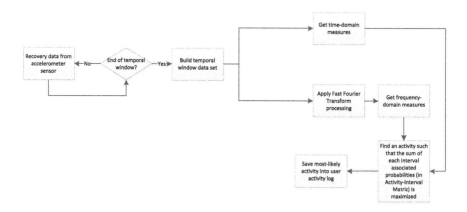

Fig. 3. Overall recognition process from data sensors

4   Method Analysis

Once exposed the bases of the developed activities recognition algorithm, an analysis of the new proposal was performed. To do this, the new development was compared with a recognition system widely used based on neural network. In this case, both learning and recognition was performed by continuous methods.

The test process was conducted in a Google Nexus One for a group of 10 users. Notably, the activity habits of these users were radically different, since 5 of them were under 30 years while the rest were older than this age. For this purpose, a document was delivered to each user for describing the activity performed, start time and end time.

Finally, the learning process consisted on the performing of each activity recognized by the system for a time of 6 minutes. As for the recognition process, users were followed over a period of 72 hours.

Moreover, the energy consumption and the processing cost of the system when it is working on a mobile device are considered. In this case, the conclusion reached is that the method based on Ameva reduces the computational cost of the system by about 50% (see Figure 4. The time needed to process a time window by using nueral networks methods is 1.2 seconds, while, for the Ameva-based method is 0.6 seconds.

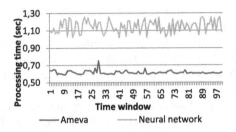

Fig. 4. Processing time of the Ameva and neural network methods on the device

As can be seen in 5, Ameva battery consumption is lower than neural networks. For the first one, the battery lifetime is close to 25 hours while for the last one, it's only 16 hours. In the comparison can be observed the battery lifetime for decision tree but the main problem of this method, based on statistics chosen, is the low accuracy, not higher than 60%.

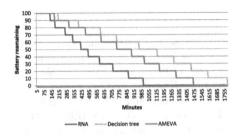

Fig. 5. Battery life for Ameva compared to neural network and decision tree methods

Based on Accuracy, Recall, Specificity, Precision, and F measure, Table 1 is presented. In this table, differences between the two methods, RNA and Ameva can be observed. Most values presented for each measure and activity show that the Ameva method performs better than RNA, especially as regards precision.

Table 1. Performance comparison by using measures of evaluation

Measure / Activity	Accuracy		Recall		Specificity		Precision		F-measure (F_1)	
	Ameva	RNA	Ameva	RNA	Ameva	RNA	Ameva	RNA	Ameva	RNA
Walk	98.77%	97.93%	97.92%	93.95%	98.91%	98.57%	93.50%	91.36%	95.66%	92.64%
Upstairs	98.93%	98.17%	95.40%	90.79%	99.43%	99.22%	96.00%	94.35%	95.70%	92.54%
Downstairs	98.64%	98.25%	95.20%	92.68%	99.04%	98.89%	91.95%	90.62%	93.55%	91.64%
Cycle	99.32%	99.03%	96.13%	95.67%	99.73%	99.47%	97.91%	95.89%	97.01%	95.78%
Immobile	98.69%	99.50%	94.57%	97.37%	99.42%	99.88%	96.60%	99.29%	95.58%	98.32%

5   Conclusions

In this work, a recognition system based only on a smartphone and, optionally, a wireless device is presented obtaining very good results. It should be noted that the system does not have communication with a server, thus it does not affect too much to de battery duration life.

Also, the Ameva discretization algorithm has been modified in order to improved the accuracy to obtain best results as the last implemented system. It has therefore been possible to achieve an average accuracy of 98% for the recognition of 7 types of activities.

In contrast, the number of activities that the system can recognize is limited, because working only with accelerometer and barometer limits the number of system variables that can be used, that it can cause that the correlation between these variables tends to be high.

Acknowledgments. This research is partially supported by the projects of the Spanish Ministry of Economy and Competitiveness ARTEMISA (TIN2009-14378-C02-01) and Simon (TIC-8052) of the Andalusian Regional Ministry of Economy.

References

1. Ravi, N., Dandekar, N., Mysore, P., Littman, M.: Activity recognition from accelerometer data. In: Proceedings of the National Conference on Artificial Intelligence, vol. 20, p. 1541. AAAI Press, MIT Press, Menlo Park, Cambridge (2005)
2. Hong, Y., Kim, I., Ahn, S., Kim, H.: Activity recognition using wearable sensors for elder care. In: Second International Conference on Future Generation Communication and Networking, vol. 2, pp. 302–305. IEEE (2008)
3. Brezmes, T., Gorricho, J.-L., Cotrina, J.: Activity recognition from accelerometer data on a mobile phone. In: Omatu, S., Rocha, M.P., Bravo, J., Fernández, F., Corchado, E., Bustillo, A., Corchado, J.M. (eds.) IWANN 2009, Part II. LNCS, vol. 5518, pp. 796–799. Springer, Heidelberg (2009)
4. Lepri, B., Mana, N., Cappelletti, A., Pianesi, F., Zancanaro, M.: What is happening now? Detection of activities of daily living from simple visual features. Personal and Ubiquitous Computing 14(8), 749–766 (2010)
5. Bicocchi, N., Mamei, M., Zambonelli, F.: Detecting activities from body-worn accelerometers via instance-based algorithms. Pervasive and Mobile Computing 6(4), 482–495 (2010)
6. Paoli, R., Fernández-Luque, F., Zapata, J.: A system for ubiquitous fall monitoring at home via a wireless sensor network and a wearable mote. Expert Systems with Applications (2011)
7. Kwapisz, J., Weiss, G., Moore, S.: Activity recognition using cell phone accelerometers. ACM SIGKDD Explorations Newsletter 12(2), 74–82 (2011)
8. Altun, K., Barshan, B., Tunçel, O.: Comparative study on classifying human activities with miniature inertial and magnetic sensors. Pattern Recognition 43(10), 3605–3620 (2010)
9. Reddy, S., Mun, M., Burke, J., Estrin, D., Hansen, M., Srivastava, M.: Using mobile phones to determine transportation modes. ACM Transactions on Sensor Networks 6(2), 13 (2010)
10. Fuentes, D., Gonzalez-Abril, L., Angulo, C., Ortega, J.: Online motion recognition using an accelerometer in a mobile device. Expert Systems with Applications 39(3), 2461–2465 (2012)

11. Cuberos, F., Ortega, J., Velasco, F., González, L.: Qsi-alternative labelling and noise sensitivity. In: 17th International Workshop on Qualitative Reasoning (2003)
12. Gonzalez-Abril, L., Cuberos, F., Velasco, F., Ortega, J.: Ameva: An autonomous discretization algorithm. Expert Systems with Applications 36(3), 5327–5332 (2009)
13. Kurgan, L., Cios, K.: Caim discretization algorithm. IEEE Transactions on Knowledge and Data Engineering 16(2), 145–153 (2004)
14. Álvarez García, J.A., Barsocchi, P., Chessa, S., Salvi, D.: Evaluation of localization and activity recognition systems for ambient assisted living: The experience of the 2012 evaal competition. Journal of Ambient Intelligence and Smart Environments 5(1), 119–132 (2013)
15. Nergui, M., Yoshida, Y., Gonzalez, J., Koike, Y., Sekine, M., Yu, W.: Human motion tracking and measurement by a mobile robot. In: 7th International Conference on Intelligent Unmanned Systems (2011)
16. Hong, J.H., Ramos, J., Dey, A.K.: Understanding physiological responses to stressors during physical activity. In: Proceedings of the 2012 ACM Conference on Ubiquitous Computing, pp. 270–279. ACM (2012)
17. Li, N., Crane, M., Ruskin, H.J.: Automatically detecting "significant events" on sensecam. Ercim News 2011(87) (2011)
18. Wolf, C., Mille, J., Lombardi, E., Celiktutan, O., Jiu, M., Baccouche, M., Dellandréa, E., Bichot, C.E., Garcia, C., Sankur, B.: The liris human activities dataset and the icpr 2012 human activities recognition and localization competition. Technical Report LIRIS RR-2012-004, Laboratoire d'Informatique en Images et Systmes d'Information, INSA de Lyon, France (2012)
19. Sagha, H., Digumarti, S.T., del Millan, J., Chavarriaga, R., Calatroni, A., Roggen, D., Troster, G.: Benchmarking classification techniques using the opportunity human activity dataset. In: 2011 IEEE International Conference on Systems, Man and Cybernetics, pp. 36–40. IEEE (2011)
20. Kawaguchi, N., Ogawa, N., Iwasaki, Y., Kaji, K., Terada, T., Murao, K., Inoue, S., Kawahara, Y., Sumi, Y., Nishio, N.: Hasc challenge: gathering large scale human activity corpus for the real-world activity understandings. In: Proceedings of the 2nd Augmented Human International Conference, p. 27. ACM (2011)
21. Loseu, V., Jafari, R.: Power aware wireless data collection for bsn data repositories. In: 2011 International Conference on Body Sensor Networks, pp. 19–21. IEEE (2011)
22. He, Z., Jin, L.: Activity recognition from acceleration data based on discrete consine transform and svm. In: 2009 IEEE International Conference on Systems, Man and Cybernetics, pp. 5041–5044. IEEE (2009)

Human Activity Recognition Based on Multiple Kinects

Emanuela Haller, Georgiana Scarlat, Irina Mocanu, and Mihai Trăscău

University POLITEHNICA of Bucharest, Computer Science Department, Romania
{haller.emanuela,georgiana.scarlat4,irinag.mocanu,
mihai.trascau}@gmail.com

Abstract. Activity recognition is an important component for the ambient assisted living systems which perform home monitoring and assistance for elderly
people or patients with risk factors. This paper presents a prototype system for
activity recognition using information provided by four Kinects. First the posture of the supervised person is detected using a set of rules created with ID3 algorithm applied to a skeleton obtained by merging the skeletons provided by
multiple Kinects. At the same time, the interaction of the user with the objects
from the house is determined. After that, daily activities are identified using
Hidden Markov Models in which the detected postures and the object interactions are observable states. The benefit of merging the information received
from multiple Kinects together with the detection of the interaction between the
user and relevant objects from the room is the increase in accuracy for the recognized activities.

Keywords: posture recognition, daily activity recognition, Kinect, Hidden
Markov Models, smart environment.

1 Introduction

The percentage of elderly in today's societies keeps on growing. As a consequence
we are faced with the problem of supporting older adults in loss of cognitive autonomy who wish to continue living independently in their home as opposed to being
forced to live in a hospital. Smart environments have been developed in order to provide a solution to this problem. The term of Ambient Intelligence (AmI) was introduced to describe a "ubiquitous electronic environment that would pro-actively, but
sensibly and non-intrusively support people in their daily lives" [1].

The need of an intelligent house is growing fast, especially for those who wish to
live on their own. People would feel much safer at home if they knew they had a system that can, for example, detect when they fall and automatically call an emergency
service.

Also, having an organized life style is hard to achieve for most people. That is why
a system that can monitor human activities and give feedback based on those detections would be extremely helpful. For example, one could receive feedback that
he/she should cycle more often since this activity has been seldom detected in the past
period of time.

J.A. Botía et al. (Eds.): EvAAL 2013, CCIS 386, pp. 48–59, 2013.

Our goal is to build a system that recognizes activities of daily living from images captured from 4 Kinects. What sets our system apart and what we will determine an increase in detection accuracy is the fact that it merges the skeletons from strategically positioned Kinect devices, making it possible to build an accurate human model and to deal with situations in which the view is partially obstructed. In addition, the fact that object interactions of the supervised person are considered enriches the proposed model and also influences the prediction accuracy in a positive way. In the future, this component of Activities of Daily Livings recognition is intended to be used in an ambient intelligent system for elderly people or people with risk factors.

The rest of the paper is organized as follows. Section 2 presents some existing methods for human activity recognition in smart environments. Section 3 describes the proposed system used for human activity recognition. Section 4 presents the current evaluation of the proposed system. Conclusions and future works are listed in Section 5.

2   Related Work

There are many attempts to recognize human activities using a wide range of devices, such as accelerometers, cameras, wearable sensors, Kinect, cell phones, etc. Jennifer R. Kwapisz et. al describe an interesting way of detecting activities in [2]. The authors use the accelerometer from smartphones in order to extract data that is afterward used to predict an activity. The activities are about of the same complexity as those discussed in this paper (walking, jogging, sitting, etc). The learning algorithms used in this article are J48, Logistic Regression and Multilayer Perceptron, but the best overall accuracy is obtained using the last one. The major drawback of this system is the fact that the information is gathered using a wireless connection. When the wireless signals are transferred they may be blocked by obstacles such as walls, gates and human beings. The strength of wireless signals depends upon the location. They can be hindered by other electronic devices, the rate of frequency and the height from the ground. Therefore, such noise can drastically affect the performances of the system. In addition, this smart phone application consumes quite a lot of energy on a device for which energy consumption is crucial.

Another method that also uses smartphones for daily activity recognition is described by Young-Seol Lee and Sung-Bae Cho in [3]. The proposed algorithm analyses certain time-series acceleration signal using hierarchical hidden Markov models. In order to address the limitations of the memory storage and computational power of the mobile devices, the recognition models are designed hierarchy as actions and activities. A sequence of actions is used as input for the HMM for real-time activity recognition on a mobile device without using the acceleration data directly. It can reduce the required time for calculation and can enhance the precision. The performance of this system is comparable with the one described in [2].

Although the accuracy of these two systems is quite high and the solution of incorporating wearable sensors into cell phones is ingenious, these systems are intrusive using the obtrusiveness of the wearable sensors.

Another approach made by Bi Song et. al in [4] develops methods for tracking and activity recognition using a distributed network of cameras. Processing power is distributed across the network and there is no central processor accumulating and analyzing all the data. For activity recognition, the authors derive a new consensus algorithm based on the recognized activity at each camera and the transition probabilities between various activities.

Our system detects daily activities based on image analyses in two phases: (i) the posture of the supervised person is detected using a set of rules obtained by applying the ID3 algorithm; (ii) Hidden Markov Models (HMM) are used for activity recognition – the detected postures are observable states for the HMM. Instead of a video camera we use images captured from 4 Kinect sensors. The posture recognition will be simplified by using the skeleton created from the joint positions obtained using the NiTE framework [7]. We use 4 Kinects in order to increase the accuracy of the provided skeleton. One Kinect is enough only for frontal postures. Other main differences in our model are: (i) a model of the room is created using the depth information provided by a Kinect sensor; (ii) interaction between the user and the objects from the room are used, which helps us to increase the accuracy of the recognized activities.

3   System Description

Further, we will present the architecture of our system (Fig. 1), which is composed of four Kinect devices and four software modules, as follows: Skeleton Detection Module, Posture Detection Module, Object Detection Module and Activity Recognition Module. To describe the workflow of the system, let's consider there is one user in the room. At least one of the Kinect devices will track the user and send data to the Skeleton Detection Module, which will apply fusion over the received data and determine a skeleton model for the tracked user. Also, the devices will extract RGB images of the environment, which will be forwarded by the Skeleton Detection Module to the Object Detection Module. The obtained skeleton model is also sent to the Posture Detection Module and an estimated posture of the user is computed and sent to the Activity Recognition Module, which will perform an estimation of the activity done by the tracked user, also incorporating data received from the Object Detection Module. This component will run an object detection algorithm, identifying some common objects that can be used by the user. At the same time, all the data (input, results, decision trees and HMM) is also stored in a common database, for further use.

3.1   Hardware Devices

In order to develop the application we use the infrastructure available in the ambient intelligence laboratory (AmI Lab), available at our university. The AmI Lab was developed with the purpose of describing an in-door tracking system, addressed to monitoring a single elder person [6]. In the lab there is a total of 27 equipments, grouped into 9 T-shaped keypoints numbered K1, K2, . . . , K9, each of them containing one Kinect and 2 Arduino-based sensors. The 9 keypoints (K1 – K9) were placed in our 8.5m x 4.5m room as evenly spaced as possible, given the constraints (door, windows and cabling). Their approximate layout is specified in Fig. 2.

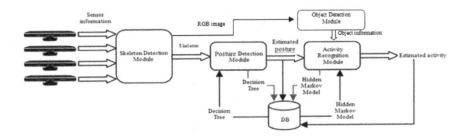

Fig. 1. System architecture

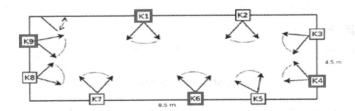

Fig. 2. Approximate layout of the 9 keypoints in the experiment room (the red ones are used in our system)

To provide an environment that is easier to set up by the user, we decided to make use of only four Kinect devices for our system. In the exceptional cases in which four Kinect devices are not enough to monitor the entire room, settings can be made to increase the number of devices.

The four devices are placed each on one of the room's walls so as to broaden the space in which the user can be detected. The height at which the devices are placed is somewhere between 200-230 cm above the floor and they are pointed slightly downward. The four devices will be placed in the room similar with devices K1, K4, K6 and K9 from Fig. 2.

3.2   Software Modules

As mentioned above, in order to detect a person in a complex environment, where different objects can interfere between the person and the Kinect device, we choose to use four different sensors, strategically positioned, in order to obtain a full body representation. The skeleton of the user will be determined by 15 body joints (Fig. 3).

Skeleton Detection Module. The first module, the Skeleton Detection Module consists of 5 sub-modules, 4 *Acquisition Sub-modules* (one for each Kinect device) and a *Central Sub-module* (Fig. 4).

Fig. 3. Body joints

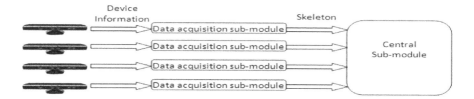

Fig. 4. Skeleton Detection Module

The *Acquisition Sub-modules* are based on the OpenNI [5] and NiTE [7] frameworks and can track all the users present in the vision area. A user is considered to be in the vision area of a Kinect device if the distance between him and the device is between 0.8 m and 3.5 m. For one user, the *Acquisition Sub-modules* will provide a skeleton model. We choose to use 4 devices, in order to track the users from different perspectives, avoiding the occlusion of some limbs. Although one device is able to track multiple users, due to the fact that our system is using four Kinect devices and each one of them will attach different IDs to the users, our system is not able to track multiple users. The generalization can be made if we force the users to wear some distinctive accessories (for example some colorful bracelets).

Each Kinect device projects its own infrared pattern in order to obtain the depth information which will be further used to compute the skeleton models. When placing more than one device in the same room, there are a set of problems that can appear, due to the inferences between the infrared laser patterns. Those inferences can cause black spots on the 3D image. This problem was approached before [8], and after reviewing previous researches and performing our own tests, we reached the conclusion that we should place the devices in such way that the optical axis would form an angle of less than 180 degrees. Also, regarding our configuration, if, for example, you choose to move K5 on the right, near the corner of the room, it will be interfering with K4, because the devices are too close.

One *Acquisition Sub-module* will provide a skeleton model of the user, represented in the world coordinate system associated with the afferent Kinect device. OpenNI applications use two different coordinate systems: the depth representation and the world representation. The world coordinates are represented in a 3D cartesian coordinate system, with the camera lens at the origin. The x axis is along a line that passes through the infrared laser, the y axis is parallel to the front face of the camera, perpendicular to the x axis, and should be perpendicular to the ground, if the camera is upright, and the z axis runs into the scene and is perpendicular to x and y axis. The skeleton model will then be forwarded to the *Central Sub-module*, along with the ID number of the Kinect device. Using the depth information, this sub-module will also provide information regarding the position of the user, if the device captures the front side of the user or his back.

The *Central Sub-module* is responsible for the data fusion process concerning the tracked users. For one user, the *Central Sub-module* will receive 4 different skeleton models, each one represented in the world coordinate system associated with the device that provided the skeleton. In order to make the fusion, we need to represent all the skeletons in the same coordinate system. This unique coordinate system will be the coordinate system associated to the room, where the y axis is perpendicular to the ground, and the x and z axis are parallel with the room walls. As we cannot determine the exact orientation of each device, we are unable to perform the direct transformation between the coordinate systems. This problem is solved by introducing a calibration process. Also, the coordinate system determined during calibration is useful for indoor localization. As we will describe later in this article, the Object Detection Module will use the location of the user within the room to determine if there are interactions between the user and the static objects represented in the room model.

Calibration is performed once, when we set up the devices in the room. This process consists in determining how each device perceives the unique coordinate system. Having this information, the *Central Sub-module* will be able to perform the coordinate system transformations. The coordinate system associated with the room is represented by an object similar to the one in Fig. 5.

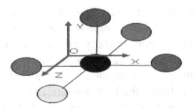

Fig. 5. Calibration object

Having this additional information for every device, the *Central Sub-module* will apply the transformation matrix to each skeleton, so all of them will be represented accordingly to the unique coordinate system. In order to perform the fusion, the 4 skeleton models obtained for one user will be merged as follows: for every joint point, we will have 4 points available and we will select those with a high grade of confidence; from those points we select a set of points, with an average distance between them less than a chosen threshold value α; the final joint point will be the average of the selected points. In conclusion, the *Central Sub-module* will provide the next layer with skeleton models with higher accuracy.

Posture Detection Module. The next principal module, the Posture Detection Module, receives as an input, from the previous module, a skeleton model of the tracked user.

Similar to the previous module, the Posture Detection Module consists of 3 sub-modules (Fig. 6), the *General Posture Detection Sub-module*, the *Coordinate System Transformation Sub-module* and the *Detailed Posture Detection Sub-module*.

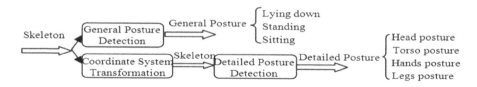

Fig. 6. Posture Detection Module

First of all, we need to determine the general posture of the user, meaning to identify the sustain point of the body, which can be the torso (for example, if the person is lying on the bed), the feet, or the backside. In order to train our system to identify those postures, we are using a supervised learning process. The training set is composed from a set of recordings, of people performing different activities (walking, lying on the bed, running, etc.). Each such recording will produce a set of frames, and each one of these frames will be labeled with the corresponding posture and sent, as a training example, to the system.

In order to classify a posture, we will use a set of attributes, which describe the posture of the body in one frame. Examples of attributes are: the angle between the y axis of the unique coordinate system (described in the previous section), and the vector between the knee and the foot; the angle between the y axis and the vector from knee to shoulder; the angle formed by the y axis and the vector between torso and shoulder, etc. We choose to consider the angles, in order to avoid the specialization of the system for people with certain dimensions. Also, by using angles we can directly determine the connection between the body posture and the floor plane, or any other relevant plane. In the same time, relations between body limbs can also be expressed using angles.

We use an extension of the ID3 algorithm [9], [10], in order to determine a decision tree that can classify the postures. A reason for not using the classic ID3 algorithm is the fact that the angles can have continuous values. Additionally, a pruning algorithm will be used, to optimize the decision tree. Consequently, the algorithm is close to the C4.5 extension.

The sustain point can be computed only relative to the coordinate system associated with the experiment room. After the general posture is determined, in order to have a more detailed look at each limb position, we choose to work in a different coordinate system representation (Fig. 7). The local coordinate system is centered in the torso joint, the positive direction of the y axis is following the neck direction and the positive direction of the z axis is perpendicular to the user torso. This representation is used because in further analysis the torso is used as landmark.

Fig. 7. Local coordinate system

The posture of each body segment is expressed relatively to body joints. As mentioned before, the principal landmark is the upper part of the torso, and the postures of body segments are expressed relative to it. For each body segment, a set of classes is defined, and each such class includes a set of similar postures of that segment. The attributes used for the classification are the angles between the body segment and the x, y and z axis. For example, if we consider the hand, after analyzing the positions of the arm and forearm, we will be able to determine if the user is holding his hand pointed forward, or backward, and if the hand is close to the body, or at a certain distance, and even if it is stretched of flexed.

The system is trained separately for each body segment, with a set of labeled frames where the user is performing several moves using a specific body segment. After the analysis of the training set, the system is able to approximate the class of a body segment, based on some classification rules.

To sum up, the Posture Detection Module will provide to the next layer an approximation of the general body posture and additional information about the posture of each body limb.

Object Detection Module. This module is responsible with recognizing a set of stationary objects from RGB images provided by the Kinect devices. We use this module in order to obtain a higher accuracy in predicting activities in which the user interacts with objects. For example, the sitting down activity includes the interaction of the user with a chair.

The module is trained to recognize some common types of chairs and beds using an OpenCV library function called Haartraining [11] (uses Viola Jones algorithm [12] to form a cascade file). The set of static objects to be recognized can be extended by obtaining the training data for the new objects and training the system to recognize them as well in the same manner as before.

This module is used during the setup stage of the system in order to create a model of the room. For now, we are interested in static objects which preserve their position in the room.

During setup, the room is scanned and the target objects are recognized within the room. Their position is marked inside a 2D map of the room (representing the projection of the objects on the room floor seen as a grid). A representation of the room model is shown in Fig. 8.

The room model created at setup is used during the activity recognition process as follows: (i) the position of the torso joint of the user is projected onto the floor; (ii) if the cell onto which the user is projected intersects or is very close to a cell representing the projection of an object, then it is considered that the user interacts with that certain object. This information is used in order to increase the accuracy of the activities done by the user and is an observable state for the HMM.

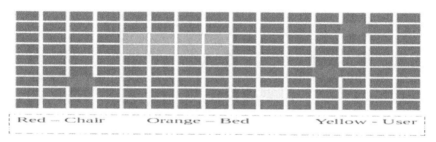

Fig. 8. Room representation

Activity Recognition Module. This module receives human position information at each frame from the Posture Detection Module and Object Detection Module and processes it in order to recognize human activities. The information received from the Posture Detection Module consists of the time stamp and the position classes with which are labeled the limbs, torso and head. The information received from the Object Detection Module is represented by a class such as: *"Chair Interaction"*, *"Bed Interaction"* or *"No Interaction"*.

Based on these sequences of information, the module uses a HMM to predict if an activity has taken place. The time interval in which the activity is performed is also determined using the timestamp with which each frame is labeled. At each frame, a certain activity with its corresponding probability is generated (this data may also be logged). Therefore, in order to determine the time interval of a certain activity, it is considered that the activity started at the moment when its probability is above a lower bound and it ends at a later moment in time, when a new activity is detected or when the probability of the current activity has gone under the lower bound. There may also be moments when none of the detectable activities takes place. These idle intervals are detected when the current predicted activities have very low probabilities. The observable variables for our HMM represent the information received from the previous modules (the classes for the torso, limbs, head and the class representing object interactions). The hidden states of the HMM are the activities that we want to recognize. So far, our system can recognize when a user is walking, lying down, sitting up and sitting down.

The model is trained in a supervised way. Also, in order to increase the accuracy of the HMM, training is done with prior knowledge of some aspects of the model. Baum–Welch algorithm [13] is used in order to learn the parameters of the HMM. The training set used at this step consists of 100 sequences of observable variables. These sequences are used to determine both transition and emission matrices.

Given the model parameters (the probabilities computed using Baum–Welch algorithm) and a sequence of observations made up to moment t (the classes for the torso, limbs, head and the class representing object interactions), this module is responsible with computing the probability of each hidden state (activity). The activity with the highest probability is chosen to describe the prediction at moment t. As described above, after having activities with their corresponding probabilities generated at each discrete moment of time, we can determine the time interval for each activity. However, our system doesn't deal with interleaved or concurrent activities for now.

As far as error handling is concerned, the Activity Recognition Module is designed to work even if there are errors within the information supplied by the Posture Detection Module, as long as they don't exceed a certain limit. This means that a large number of consecutive noise affected frames can prevent the system from successfully detecting an activity, but if there are only a few frames affected by noise, and they are scattered throughout the entire sequence of received frames, then the system can still work quite well. As discussed earlier in this paper, the system can predict that a certain activity takes place at a moment of time if its probability is above a lower bound. However, in order to deal with noise, we consider that an activity has to last a minimum amount of time for it to be valid (there are different thresholds for each detectable activity). If there are predictions of activities that last less than the inferior limit specified earlier, then they are most likely wrong. This kind of error is handled by replacing the current wrong prediction with the prediction made immediately before it. Furthermore, this module will offer feedback to the Posture Detection Module in order to increase the accuracy of its detections.

Errors can also occur because of the information received from the Object Detection Module. It is possible that a user can be projected extremely close to an object, but no interactions between the two actually occur. In such cases, the predicted activity should not be affected very much as long as the data received from the Posture Detection Module is accurate. In this case, only the activity's probability would be lower, but it would still be above the lower bound, unless the data received from the Posture Detection Module is also misclassified.

4   System Evaluation

Further, we will present the experimental results obtained by each of the software modules.

The calibration process is having a rate of success of 97%. The errors appear due to the light reflections over the surface of the calibration object. In 3% of the situations, the calibration object is not completely identified, but due to its dimensions, the introduced deviation is unnoticeable for the final results.

In order to detect the interaction of the user with different static objects, the Object Detection Module needs to determine the position of the user inside the 2D map of the room. More precisely, it needs to obtain the cell onto which the user is projected. The correct position of the user is detected in 96% of the situations. In 4% of the tested scenarios, the position is incorrectly detected due to errors introduced by the Kinect devices.

In order to detect objects of interest such as chairs and beds we have divided them into more specific categories for which we have trained individual classifiers (office chair, windsor chair, etc.). The training set for each object consists of around 4000 positive examples and 3000 negative examples. In order to evaluate the performance of this module we used about 300 testing samples per object.

The training set was realized using two subjects (one at a time), with different body structures. We built two different training sets, one for training the system in order to provide the detailed posture, and one for training the system to detect the general posture of the body, and to detect the activity of the person. As mentioned above, for the detailed posture detection, we used recordings of people making different moves with a specific body limb. For the other training set, we used recordings of people performing the following activities: walking, lying down, sitting up and sitting down.

The system was tested with three subjects, the two used for the training set and an additional one. The tests, along with the recordings for the training set were developed in the experiment room described in Fig. 2. The use of four Kinects is justified by the fact that, in our experiments, we noticed that a device may have a low accuracy in 20% of cases, but only in 5% of the cases the low accuracy is noticed at all the devices simultaneously, as the position of the user is different relative to each device.

There were no notable differences between testing on the training subjects and testing on a new subject. This proves that using the angles as attributes for classifications offers a high degree of independence from a specific body structure, offering a system able to answer correctly for every individual, without the need to train the system for that individual.

Fig. 9 presents the experimental results regarding the accuracy of the software modules:

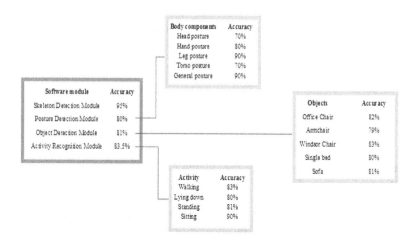

Fig. 9. Experimental results

5   Conclusions and Future Work

Human activity recognition finds application in a large set of fields, as human machine interaction, security surveillance, etc. In this paper, we present an approach with a high grade of accuracy, which can be easily implemented in different environments.

Our system provides room for further development, in more than one direction. The first approach is to increase the number of activities recognized by the system, meaning that the system will be able to recognize activities like running, cycling, etc.

Extensions can also be made in order to detect a larger number of objects relevant to the targeted activities and to be able to predict interactions not only with static objects, but also with moving ones. Another improvement can be done by increasing the number of subjects used for recording the training set, in order to avoid the specialization of the system with a certain body structures.

Also, the system can be extended in such way that it could be able to respond correctly in situations where one or more body parts are blocked from the line of sight of the Kinect devices. This can be achieved by using some advanced image processing algorithms, but if the experiment room is not properly lighted the best solution is to get use of wearable sensors.

References

1. Ramos, C., Augusto, J., Shapiro, D.: Ambient intelligence - the next step for artificial intelligence. IEEE Intelligent Systems 23(2), 15–18 (2008)
2. Kwapisz, J.R., Weiss, G.M., Moore, S.A.: Activity Recognition using Cell Phone Accelerometers. ACM SIGKDD Explorations Newsletter 12(2), 74–82 (2010)
3. Lee, Y.-S., Cho, S.-B.: Activity Recognition Using Hierarchical Hidden Markov Models on a Smartphone with 3D Accelerometer. In: Corchado, E., Kurzyński, M., Woźniak, M. (eds.) HAIS 2011, Part I. LNCS, vol. 6678, pp. 460–467. Springer, Heidelberg (2011)
4. Song, B., Kamal, A.T., Soto, C., Ding, C., Roy-Chowdhury, A.K., Farrell, J.A.: Tracking and Activity Recognition Through Consensus in Distributed Camera Networks. IEEE Transactions on Image Processing 19(10), 2564–2579 (2010)
5. OpenNI: http://www.openni.org (accessed April 2013)
6. Ismail, A.-A., Florea, A.-M.: Multimodal indoor tracking of a single elder in an AAL environment. In: van Berlo, A., Hallenborg, K., Rodríguez, J.M.C., Tapia, D.I., Novais, P. (eds.) Ambient Intelligence – Software & Applications. AISC, vol. 219, pp. 137–145. Springer, Heidelberg (2013), http://isami.usal.se
7. Nite: http://www.openni.org/files/nite (accessed April 2013)
8. Caon, M., Yue, Y., Tscherrig, J., Mugellini, E., Khaled, O.A.: Context-Aware 3D Gesture Interaction Based on Multiple Kinects. In: AMBIENT 2011: The First International Conference on Ambient Computing, Applications, Services and Technologies, pp. 7–12 (2011)
9. Quinlan, J.R.: Induction of decision trees. Machine Learning 1, 81–106 (1986)
10. Quinlan, J.R.: C4.5: Programs for Machine Learning. Morgan Kaufmann Publishers, Inc., Los Altos (1993)
11. Tutorial: OpenCV Haartraining (Rapid Object Detection with a Cascade of Boosted Clasifiers Based on Haar-like Features), http://note.sonots.com/SciSoftware/haartraining.html (accessed April 2013)
12. Viola, P., Jones, M.: Robust Real-time Object Detection, http://research.microsoft.com/en-us/um/people/viola/Pubs/Detect/violaJones_IJCV.pdf (accessed April 2013)
13. The Baum-Welch & Viterbi Algorithm, http://www.princeton.edu/~apapanic/Stochastic_Analysis_Seminar_%28Spring2011%29_files/08baumWelch.pdf (accessed April 2013)

RealTrac Technology Overview

Alex Moschevikin[1,2], Aleksandr Galov[1], Alexei Soloviev[2], Alexander Mikov[1],
Alexander Volkov[1], and Sergey Reginya[1]

[1] RTL-Service ltd.
[2] Petrozavodsk State University,
Lenin Str., 31, 185910 Petrozavodsk, Russian Federation
{alexmou,gas}@rtlservice.com, avsolov@lab127.ru,
sir.enmity@gmail.com, {avolkov,reginya}@rtlservice.com
http://www.rtlservice.com

Abstract. This paper presents the overview of the RealTrac™ technology
developed by the RTL-Service ltd. It is based on the nanoLOC (IEEE
802.15.4a) radio standard. The RealTrac™ technology features the local
positioning system including the possibility of data transfer and voice communication. Radio access is provided by gateway units connected by wired
network to a system server. Repeater units are used to increase the radio
coverage area. Both gateway and repeater units serve as access points in
a system. Channels for voice communication are supported by the Asterisk PBX software installed at the system server. Mobile handheld units
periodically enter into active state and initiate the time-of-flight (ToF)
ranging. Access points measure received signal strength (RSS) of the incoming radio signal. ToF and RSS data is processed by the server using
a particle filter within localization algorithms. The following information
is taken into consideration: ToF, RSS, structure of the building, air pressure value and inertial measurement unit data. The developed protocols
for the communication in the system are discussed as well.

Keywords: local positioning system, indoor navigation, RTLS, Bayesian
filter, particle filter, nanoLOC, IEEE 802.15.4a, time-of-flight, received
signal strength, LOS, NLOS, RealTrac.

1 Introduction

Recently, research and business communities show a great interest in the Local
Positioning System (LPS) technology. Unlike the Global Positioning Systems
(GPS, Galileo, GLONASS, QZSS), LPS systems allow indoors localization. In
order to locate an object within a certain area, a wireless infrastructure needs to
be installed. As a rule, indoors, the localization accuracy depends on the spatial
density of anchor nodes. Those anchors are used to measure distances to mobile
nodes.

Real-time positioning systems are based on wireless networks which can
utilize different methods of distance measurement: Time-of-Flight (ToF), Angle-
of-Arrival (AoA) and Received Signal Strength (RSS). Methods based on Time-of-
Arrival (ToA), Time-Difference-of-Arrival (TDoA), Round-Trip-Time (RTT) are

J.A. Botía et al. (Eds.): EvAAL 2013, CCIS 386, pp. 60–71, 2013.

referred to the ToF methods group. First two methods (ToA and TDoA) do require system time synchronization between all nodes in the system, whereas the RTT method does not. Obviously, distance measurements based on the RSS are relatively inaccurate, especially in a case of substantial distances between nodes. However, knowing of the RSS value is very important for applications with room-level accuracy indoors: room walls create a drop in a signal strength, which is used to reliably determine the room where the mobile object is in. This technique is widely used in RSS patterns methods [1,2].

Along with the localization capability, wireless networks provide data communications channels between nodes. Commercial LPSs use various radio technologies: Wi-Fi, ZigBee, UWB, nanoLOC, NFC RFID, etc. This paper presents an overview of the RealTrac™technology developed by the RTL-Service ltd. It is based on the nanoLOC (IEEE 802.15.4a) radio standard. The RealTrac™technology combines good data transfer rates with low power consumption of radio devices, location estimation and voice communication feature at the same time.

The rest of this paper is organized as follows. Section 2 describes architecture of the RealTrac™technology; technical characteristics of devices used; data transfer protocols for communication between radio modules in the system and between a client and a server. Section 3 is devoted to the applied location estimation algorithms based primarily on the particle filter. ToF and RSS values, building structure, constraints on object velocity and data acquired from the embedded inertial measurement unit (IMU) are taken into a consideration. The opportunity of using the precise air pressure sensor is utilized for the floor identification and for the estimation of the relative height. Those features are based on the atmospheric pressure data of all devices in the system. Section 4 concludes the development work and briefly describes possible applications of the described technology and defines future development directions.

2   RealTrac™Technology Description

2.1   Network Structure and Operation Algorithms

The RealTrac™radio system is based on the nanoLOC communication standard (introduced by Nanotron Technologies GmbH, Germany). The main feature of this standard is the automatic distance measurement using the Time-of-Flight method. The measured distances between fixed nodes and a mobile node are used to estimate the location of the mobile object. The brief summary of the nanoLOC radio specifications [3] is presented in Table 1.

The RealTrac™system components can be divided into two parts: hardware and software. The hardware part includes all physical devices (intercoms, gateways, repeaters, servers, switches, etc.). All devices are uniquely identified by their MAC addresses. The software part includes client software communicating with a system server.

The network diagram of the system is presented in Fig. 1. The radio coverage area is formed by access points (AP). They operate in either gateway or repeater

Table 1. NanoLOC radio standard specifications

Parameter	Value
Frequency range	2.4 ... 2.48 GHz, ISM, unlicensed
Frequency band	80 MHz, 1 channel (optional: 3 channels of 22 MHz)
RF signal encoding	chirp modulation
Bit rate	1 Mbit/s
TX power	100 mW (20 dBm), software control
Medium access method	primarily CSMA (TDMA is possible)
The accuracy of ranging	up to 1 meter
The method of ranging	propagation delay, round-trip time
Range of reliable connection between access points	up to 1500 meters (outdoors, directed antennas), 50-70 meters (indoors, through several walls)
Range of reliable connection between an access point and a mobile node	up to 400 meters (outdoors), 50 meters (indoors, through several walls)

mode. The gateways are connected to the server via Ethernet cable network (via switches). They act as a bridge between the wired and wireless segments of the system. All data packets from the wireless part of the network are redirected into the wired part and vice versa. When the AP is not connected by a wired connection to the Ethernet network, it switches to the repeater mode automatically. In this particular mode it retransmits all incoming broadcast traffic back into the wireless segment, therefore increasing the radio coverage area. The AP works as a reference point in positioning (as an anchor) in both gateway and repeater modes.

A mobile handheld device is called intercom, since it provides voice communication. The intercom is set into a power saving mode for the larger part of a duty cycle. In the active state it is in the listening mode and collecting the information regarding neighbor units (MAC addresses of gateways, receivers and other intercom units). The intercom receives copies of the own packets resented by repeaters and obtains their MAC addresses. The list of neighbors is constantly updated. Normally this list is never empty for duty cycles less than 10 seconds. For the larger periods some entries become outdated and they are deleted from the list.

The intercom performs ranging measurements to several anchors just after waking up. The ranging results (if any) are broadcasted by the intercom in a so-called blink packet. This packet is received by gateway(s) and then redirected to the system server. If there are no gateways around, this packet is delivered to the system server by repeaters, which retransmit the received broadcast packet.

The server analyzes the blink packet and issues a set of commands to a number of gateways to execute additional ranging to intercoms if needed. There was developed number of adaptive algorithms used to determine the required number of additional ToF distance measurements to satisfy the sufficient accuracy. This centralized control of ranging queue increases the efficiency of CSMA algorithm [4].

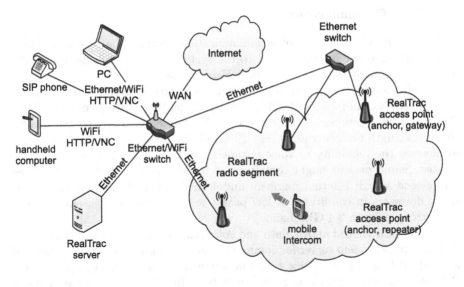

Fig. 1. RealTrac™ technology network diagram

For large covered areas the server may control several non-intersecting radio zones and assign the dedicated queue to each radio zone. All the obtained ranging data is processed and the location of the mobile node is determined.

The RealTrac™ technology does not directly limit the maximum number of used mobile devices. This number depends on the intercoms duty cycle and on the volume of generated data traffic in the wireless segment.

The maximum payload size of the nanoLOC data frame is 128 bytes. Therefore the largest frame transmission, including a preamble, duration of data radio frame, inter-frame gap and the acknowledgement frame, lasts approximately 1.4 ms at 1 Mbps (chirp/symbol duration is 1 us) speed. The NanoLOC radio uses RTT method for the ranging. To calculate the distance, three data frames together with following acknowledgements should be sent. This cycle lasts approximately 3-7 ms. The average value of the time differences between the data frame and the acknowledgement frame at local and remote sides corresponds to the measured distance.

Single location estimation assumes up to 4-5 ranging procedures to be executed. Accordingly, the system is able to process not more than 20-25 locations per 1 second taking into consideration a certain reserved space in the radio bandwidth. The system server can adjust the intercoms duty cycle in the range between 0.3 second to 3 minutes by sending a distinct command.

The simplified rule for the maximum quantity of nodes calculation is the following. If the intercoms duty cycle is 1 second, then the network can operate only with 20 intercom units; if duty cycle is 10 seconds, maximum units quantity increases up to 200. For 1200 mobile nodes the duty cycle is 20 seconds, however location estimations are done only once per 3 minutes.

2.2 Voice Communication

The intercom unit supports voice communication feature. That allows to make phone calls to other intercoms and to the system server in full duplex mode. Also it can be used like a radio set in half-duplex mode.

The bitrate of the one-way voice channel is approximately 8 kbps. Uncompressed voice is sampled at 16 bit quantization depth and frequency of 8 kHz. The hardware compression according to G.729A is applied. Sound packets by 100 bytes length are generated every 20 ms (50 packets per 1 second). In order to increase the reliability of voice channels additional redundancy was implemented. Sound packets might contain up to 5 sound fragments by 20 ms of the compressed sound: 1 actual fragment and 4 outdated. Redundancy level adaptively decreases in conditions of low packet loss and increases in environment with strong noise in 2.4 GHz band.

As it was mentioned above, data and voice packets from handheld devices are directed to the system server for communication and data acquisition, processed and stored (see Fig. 2). Voice communication is provided by the open source PBX Asterisk software, featuring SIP telephony functionality. Software PBX is responsible for redirecting calls to other intercom units and external soft-phone clients. If the server is equipped with the special telephony adapter, then calls can be redirected even to POTS or cellular phone network. Any client software which supports G.729A codec might be used both on handheld computers and laptops to accept and place voice calls from and to intercoms. If the soft-phone does not support G.729A codec, Asterisk should be configured to transcode the voice traffic.

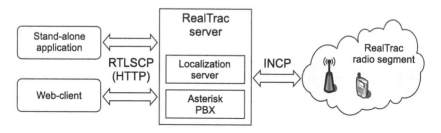

Fig. 2. The RealTrac™ technology communication diagram

When the intercom unit is moving while the voice call, system server provides automatic roaming within the network. The server sends sound packets through the most appropriate gateway unit (the nearest to the intercom).

2.3 INCP

The RealTrac™ uses the unique protocol INCP (Inter-Nano-Com Protocol), developed for the communication between devices and software modules. The asymmetrical protocol recognizes a dedicated system server with the certain roles and several clients with a limited number of functions. Every INCP message is encapsulated in either UDP packet (over Ethernet network) or nanoLOC frame (over wireless network).

The brief information on INCP headers is presented in Table 2.

Table 2. INCP message structure

Offset	15	14	13	12	11	10	9	8	7	6	5	4	3	2	1	0
0	Ver[4]				Len[12]											
2	Type[8]								Hops[8]							
4 6	PacketID[32]															
8	Reserved								B	R	R	R	DevType[4]			
10	TxPower[8]								RxPower[8]							
12 14 16	DeviceID[48]															
18	Message payload[...]															

Some fields in this table need to be explained. Due to the broadcast nature of wireless traffic, INCP messages may be delivered to the server via different routes. Consequently, the server may receive several copies of the same INCP message. Data fields *PacketID* and *DeviceID* provide a way to distinguish replicas of different INCP messages from each other. On one hand, the system server must recognize duplicates of the original message and prevent from repeated processing. On the other hand, those replicas may be useful for discovering network structure of the system. *PacketID* is a 32 bit integer number, which is unique across messages of certain device during certain interval (at least 10 sec). RealTrac™ devices use internal clock counter as a *PacketID* value. *DeviceID* is a 48 bit integer number, which corresponds to MAC address of the given device. The system server inserts the MAC address of the destination device into this field.

The message contains other fields, which are used for investigation process of the network structure in general and for the position calculation of the origin device – in particular: *Hops*, *RxPower*, *TxPower*. The value in the *Hops* field is incremented when the message passes gateway or repeater units on its way to the system server. Accordingly, the value 0 may be found in the messages originated by gateways. The value 1 may be found in a message from a mobile device when it is located in the range of a certain gateway. The values greater than 1 may be found in a message from a device, which is out of a range of any gateway, and thus the message was relayed by repeaters at least once.

The value in the *TxPower* field corresponds to the RF output power of the origin device. The value in the *RxPower* field corresponds to the received signal strength at the first repeater or gateway. These two values help to evaluate path loss between two devices.

All the INCP message features may be separated into three categories.

- Voice communication (CALL, BYE, SND_PACKET, BANDWIDTH_REQUEST).
- Firmware updates (TFTP_PACKET).
- Status acquisition and configuration (ALIVE, PARAMETER).

The ALIVE message may contain series of blocks, for example: *LOCATION*, *VERSION*, *CONFIG*, *STATE* and *IMU* blocks. *LOCATION* block is used to deliver ToF, RSS and IMU data to the server.

Some parameters of the device may be changed by the system server. It may set RF output power, status reporting interval, ring and voice volume by sending the PARAMETER message. Also, the server may turn the device off or suspend / resume IMU function.

2.4   RealTrac™ API

The RealTrac™server can communicate with software clients through web protocols (see Fig. 2). The Real Time Location System Communication Protocol (RtlsCP) – the public API, was developed for this purpose. Requests and responses format is based on JSON notation.

RtlsCP covers most common features of all RTL systems and provides necessary services for handling the RealTrac™hardware and visualization. The common API provides the following data.

- Anchors and mobile nodes list.
- Anchors and mobile nodes real time locations data.
- Anchors and mobile nodes parameters and statuses.
- KML files for visualization.

KML formatted files were used in RtlsCP since KML become natively be supported by both Google Maps and Google Earth applications. RtlsCP can operate with either relative (x, y, height) or absolute (latitude, longitude, altitude) coordinates.

3   Positioning Technique Overview

3.1   Localization Server

All the measured data, including ToF, RSS, air pressure and IMU data is processed by the localization server. Initially, the air pressure data is used for altitude calculation. Next, the floor in a building is determined and the corresponding 2D map is identified. After that, all measurements and the 2D map are used for the estimation of a mobile node position (x, y coordinates) on the specified floor. Finally mobile node 3D location (x,y,z) is sent to software clients through the web using RtlsCP.

3.2   Location Algorithms Implementation

To combine all available sources of information for accurate positioning the Bayesian filtering [5] was used. The main goal of this method is to give an optimal estimation of a target location $\hat{x}_t$ which is characterized by pdf $P(X_t)$. By Bayes theorem

$$P(X_{t_n}|Y_{t_1,\ldots,t_n}) = \frac{P(Y_{t_n}|X_{t_n}) * P(X_{t_n})}{P(Y_{t_n})}. \tag{1}$$

In this equation a posterior probability $P(X_{t_n}|Y_{t_1,\ldots,t_n})$ represents the estimated pdf of the system state. The likelihood $P(Y_{t_n}|X_{t_n})$ refers to the measurements model. The vector of distances $R_n = [r_{B_1},\ldots,r_{B_k}]$ and the vector of signal strengths $RSS_n = [rss_{B_1},\ldots,rss_{B_k}]$ measured at each time moment t_n between the set of anchors $B_1,\ldots,B_k$ and a mobile node (target) are used for the likelihood calculation. The prior $P(X_t)$ represents the target model. For the prior calculation it is possible to use the information about the motion model, IMU data, and structure of the building. The $P(Y_{t_n})$ is used as the normalization coefficient.

The filter is based on a recursive estimation of the system state X_{t_n} by noisy measurements Y_{t_n} at time t_n taking into account all previous measurements $Y_{t_1,\ldots,t_{n-1}}$. The system state X_{t_n} consists of the target coordinates x_n and velocity v_n. The Y_{t_n} refers to the data obtained from ranging measurements.

In the ongoing work particle filter was applied for the location calculation. Particle filter is the implementation of the Bayesian filtering using the Sequential Monte-Carlo Method. In this method system state is represented by the set of random samples or particles with corresponding weights. This particle system is located, weighted and propagated recursively according to the Bayesian rule [6].

At each moment the pdf is characterized by the set of particles $x_t^{(i)}, i = 1..N$, with weights $w_t^{(i)}, i = 1..N$, where particle $x_t^{(i)}$ corresponds to the system state and includes information about target coordinates and velocities, $w_t^{(i)}$ is the non-negative weight of the corresponding particle. The weights are normalized the way, so that $\sum w_t^{(i)} = 1$.

The algorithm of the particle filter consists of several phases: initialization, propagation, weights calculation, resampling, and state estimation. During the initialization the weights are uniformly distributed in the area of the intersection of circles corresponded to the measured distances (Fig. 3), thus $w^{(i)} = \frac{1}{N}$.

In propagation phase the position of a particle is calculated with the use of the following motion model equation

$$x_n = x_{n-1} + (v_{n-1} \cdot t), \tag{2}$$

where x_n and x_{n-1} denote to coordinates of the target location at the corresponding time moments n and $n-1$, v_{n-1} is the vector of the target velocity at the moment $n-1$, and t is the time interval between time moments n and $n-1$. The vector v of the target velocity consists of two components v_r, and v_α. The components change consequently that $v_{rn} = v_{rn-1} + \Delta v_r$, and

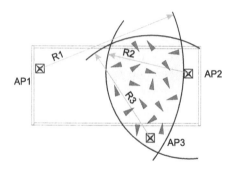

Fig. 3. Initial particles, generated inside the circles intersection area

$v_{an} = v_{an-1} + \Delta v_\alpha$. $\Delta v_r = N(0, \sigma_{v_r})$ is normally distributed random noise with deviation σ_{v_r}, corresponding to the possible changes in speed of a target, and $\Delta v_\alpha = R(-\alpha, \alpha)$ is the uniformly distributed random noise, corresponding to the possible changes in target direction.

The information about v_r and v_α is gotten from IMU or is chosen corresponding to the motion model. The errors δv_r and δv_α are chosen empirically.

The structure of the building information is used for increasing positioning accuracy [7]. If the particle during its motion crosses the wall (which is impossible for real target motion), it is removed from the current set (see Fig. 4).

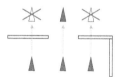

Fig. 4. Particle propagation restricted due to building structure

The source ToF and RSS data is used to recalculate the weight of each particle. The procedure of the weights calculation corresponds to the calculation of likelihood in (1). At this step it is possible to combine (or fuse) the results of different weighting algorithms. Let indexes $A_1, \ldots, A_m$ correspond to different algorithms, and let $w_{A_j}^{(i)}$ be the weight of i-th particle calculated from algorithm A_j. Then after calculation of weights for each particle for each algorithm the final particle weight is calculated as

$$w^{(i)} = \frac{\prod_{k=1}^m w_{A_k}^{(i)}}{\sum_{j=1}^N \prod_{k=1}^m w_{A_k}^{(j)}}. \tag{3}$$

In the ongoing work the RSS pattern matching algorithm [8] was used as the basic algorithm for likelihood calculation $P(Y_t|X_t)$ since it demonstrates better accuracy in the case of the signal shadowing and NLOS conditions [1].

After weights calculation the multinomial resampling algorithm was used [6] to avoid the degeneracy problem (in case if after several steps the weights of majority of particles become zero).

Finally, the system state is calculated as the weighted sum of resampled particles:

$$\hat{x} = \sum_{i=1}^{N} w^{(i)} x^{(i)}. \tag{4}$$

3.3 Pressure Sensor Usage

Every RealTrac^{TM}device is equipped with the Bosch BMP085 air pressure sensor. Therefore both stationary and mobile nodes measure absolute air pressure and send results to the system server.

The BMP085 features 4 sampling modes and has absolute accuracy ±100 Pa and 1 Pa resolution of the output data. According to preliminary experiments with this sensor, which was set in high and ultra-high resolution modes, the peak-to-peak pressure values do not exceed the range of 25-30 Pa (2.5-3 m) [9]. Thus it is possible to use the sensor for floor identification in a multistory building and even for localization of an object on inter-floor places.

The applicability of the pressure sensor to measure the changes of relative height is demonstrated in Fig. 5. At zero time moment two devices were at the same height (on the floor). Approximately at the 43-th second one of the devices (altitude values marked as rhombi) was raised to the height of 1.5 m. Two curves were obtained by the simplest 5-point un-weighted smoothing. The altitude in meters was calculated using the international barometric formula with the measured pressure and the pressure at the sea level at 1013.25 hPa.

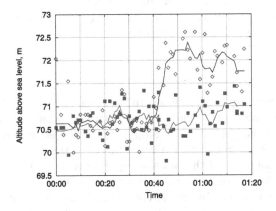

Fig. 5. Altitude changes registration

3.4   IMU-Based Localization

The developed solution assumes that an IMU could be installed in any point at the persons body. The IMU has 3-axis accelerometer and 3-axis gyroscope. The accelerometer is active on permanent basis. In order to preserve the power, the gyroscope is turned on only in case of the person motion or walking process is detected.

The IMU-based solution includes three modules: distance, orientation and trajectory calculation modules.

The first module calculates the total travelled distance by counting number of steps and estimation of each steps length. The number of steps is calculated with the high accuracy, more than 98%. Algorithms displayed excellent performance with no regard to orientation of the device, speed of walk or other person specific parameters. For step length estimation several methods were tested. The following formula [10] was used as the most efficient: $L_{step} = K \sqrt[4]{a_{max} - a_{min}}$. The calibration constant value was chosen empirically.

To represent the orientation of the device the quaternions were used. To avoid heavy calculations while getting the attitude, the complementary filter was applied [11]. The heading direction is calculated as a mean of 2-dimensional vector using quaternion observations.

The position update was performed at each foot step. When the new step is detected, the system acquires the step length and the step heading direction. Both the step length and the heading direction are served into the path restoration module. Those values are multiplied and new position point is added to the trajectory. Those calculations are performed by the internal MCU of handheld devices. Compressed trajectory data is sent to the server within the INCP `ALIVE` message.

During the experiments on evaluation of IMU accuracy, a researcher walked along the corridors of O-shaped building with a perimeter about 270 m and then returned to the starting point. The computed return position was compared with the real one. The parameter Return Position Error (RPE) for multiple tests did not exceed 3% of the total travelled distance.

4   Conclusion

The RealTrac^{TM}technology can be successfully applied for the Local Positioning Systems development and for providing voice communication over the wireless sensors network infrastructure. As an example, a pilot project in a collaboration with Intelmine ltd. (Russian Federation) was started in the year of 2012. It was devoted to the development of the positioning, data and voice communication system in mines. Specific restrictions on intrinsic safety were applied to the equipment. The first trial results at the coal mine "Polysayevskaya" displayed high reliability of the technology. The RealTrac^{TM}can also be successfully used in hospitals, in logistics for the large industrial areas, in hotel business, etc.

It should be noted that the current implementation of IMU does not require user calibration and works robust with any speed of walk. However, it accumulates yaw error and this error could not be removed easily without additional information. Thus one of the directions of future development will be discovering new algorithms of the IMU-based data fusion with the RSS/ToF based data and the building structure in the localization engine. This work will also include further modification of the particle filter.

Another area for the development concerns the altitude estimation accuracy. The authors team plan to investigate cooperative algorithms for calculation of relative height providing accuracy better than 0.5 m.

Acknowledgments. The research work described in this publication was ordered by the RTL-Service ltd., and was supported by the Petrozavodsk State University (within the program of the Strategic Development Program of PetrSU) and the Education and Science Ministry of the Russian Federation and the Economic Development Ministry of the Republic of Karelia (Russian Federation).

References

1. Chandrasekaran, G., Ergin, M., Yang, J., Liu, S., Chen, Y., Gruteser, M., Martin, R.: Empirical Evaluation of the Limits on Localization Using Signal Strength: Beyond Cramer-Rao Bounds. In: Proc. of IEEE SECON, pp. 1–9 (June 2009)
2. Elnahrawy, E., Li, X., Martin, R.: The Limits of Localization Using Signal Strength: A Comparative Study. In: Proc. of IEEE SECON, pp. 406–414 (October 2004)
3. Nanotron Technology GmbH, http://www.nanotron.com
4. Galov, A., Moschevikin, A., Soloviev, A.: Reducing radio bandwidth in nanoLOC-based wireless networks through selecting correct base stations for ranging. Special Issue on "Wireless Systems" of the International Journal of Computing 10(4), 358–366 (2011)
5. Fox, D., Hightower, J., Liao, L., Schulz, D., Borriello, G.: Bayesian Filtering for Location Estimation. IEEE Pervasive Computing, 24–33 (September 2003)
6. Chen, Z.: Bayesian Filtering: From Kalman Filters to Particle Filters, and Beyond. Technical Report McMasters University, Hamilton, ON (2003)
7. Widyawan, Klepal, M., Pesch, D.: A Bayesian Approach for RF-Based Indoor Localization. In: Proc. of the 4th International Symposium on Wireless Communication Systems, pp. 133–137 (October 2007)
8. Galov, A., Moschevikin, A., Voronov, R.: Combination of RSS localization and ToF ranging for increasing positioning accuracy indoors. In: Proc. of the 11th International Conference on ITS Telecommunications (ITST), pp. 299–304 (2011)
9. Moschevikin, A., Voronov, R., Galov, A., Soloviev, A.: Using Pressure Sensors for Floor Identification in Wireless Sensors Networks. In: Proc. of the IEEE 1st International Symposium on Wireless Systems (IDAACS-SWS), Offenburg, Germany, pp. 2–6 (September 2012)
10. Weinberg, H.: Using the ADXL202 in Pedometer and Personal Navigation Applications. Application note AN-602, Analog Devices Inc. (2002)
11. Mahony, R., Hamel, T., Pflimlin, J.-M.: Nonlinear Complementary Filters on the Special Orthogonal Group. IEEE Transactions on Automatic Control 53(5), 1203–1218 (2008)

Enhancements to the LOCOSmotion Person Tracking System

Ngewi Fet, Marcus Handte,
Stephan Wagner, and Pedro José Marrón

Networked Embedded Systems Group
University of Duisburg-Essen and
Locoslab GmbH, Germany
{ngewi.fet,marcus.handte,stephan.j.wagner,pjmarron}@uni-due.de

Abstract. Indoor localization is a key component in context-aware applications and assisted-living technologies. In prior work, we presented the design and implementation of the LOCOSmotion indoor person tracking system that uses Wireless LAN fingerprinting and accelerometer-based dead-reckoning [5]. In this paper, we analyze the optimization potentials of the previous implementation LOCOSmotion and propose modifications and enhancements which address them. In particular, we focus on reducing the time and cost of deployment, as well as on a number of refinements to improve the localization precision. Aside from optimization of the calibration tools and underlying localization algorithms, the refinements also encompass the use of feedback provided by the domestic robotics (domotics) in the Living Lab to improve the overall system performance.

Keywords: Localization, Tracking, Pervasive Computing, LOCOSmotion.

1 Introduction

Pervasive computing envisions seamless and distraction-free support for tasks by means of context-aware applications. In many of these applications, knowledge about the user's location is a key requirement. However the use of the Global Positioning System for location determination is limited by the unavailability of its signals in indoor environments. Hence, in recent years, much attention has been focused on developing alternative solutions for indoor localization. Rapid advances in wireless communication technologies and the miniaturization of consumer electronics have led to an increase in the deployment and accessibility of wireless local area networks (WLAN) and WLAN-capable mobile devices. This presents an opportunity to leverage and reuse the existing infrastructure for the development of localization systems without incurring extra costs for setup and maintenance. Also, most of the mobile devices today come packed with a plethora of other sensors such as accelerometers and gyroscopes which make them ideal for use as location sensing platforms.

J.A. Botía et al. (Eds.): EvAAL 2013, CCIS 386, pp. 72–82, 2013.
© Springer-Verlag Berlin Heidelberg 2013

In previous work [5], we described the design and implementation of LO-COSmotion, a WLAN-based indoor localization system. The basic operational principle of LOCOSmotion is similar to RADAR [2] in that it uses WLAN-based fingerprinting for location estimation. However, in contrast to RADAR, LOCOSmotion additionally performs accelerometer-based dead-reckoning in order to improve the localization precision while guaranteeing a minimum location update rate of 2Hz.

In this paper, we describe the implementation of several optimizations to the LOCOSmotion system based on our experiences during the EvAAL 2012 competition. To evaluate the optimizations, we present the results of a number of experiments that we performed in our laboratory at the University of Duisburg-Essen. The optimizations focus on a significant reduction of the calibration effort by providing better tools for the initial training, as well as improvements to the robustness of the dead-reckoning algorithm. Furthermore, we enhance the LOCOSmotion system to intelligently take advantage of any domotic event notifications which may be provided in order to increase the accuracy of the system.

The rest of this paper is broken down as follows; in the next section, we discuss related work in the field of indoor localization and then briefly outline the basic architecture of LOCOSmotion system in the Section 3. In Section 4, we outline the potential optimizations and propose enhancements which address them. Section 5 presents an evaluation of the impact of the optimizations on the performance of the system. Finally, we conclude the paper with a short summary.

2 Related Work

Many different systems have been developed for indoor localization and they employ different technologies to perform location estimation. Vision-based systems make use of cameras and computer vision for location estimation [6]. Other indoor localization systems have been developed on the basis of infrared light [19], ultrasound [20], or magnetic signals [9]. However, since LOCOSmotion is using RF technology as basis for localization, we are focusing on RF-based systems in the following.

One of the earliest systems that uses WLAN fingerprinting for indoor localization is RADAR [2]. In RADAR, a fingerpint is a tuple of location coordinates and signal strengths of visible WLAN networks. In a training phase, WLAN fingerprints are collected at all locations in the target area to form a radio map. During localization, WLAN scans are matched against this radio map to estimate the location of the user. As described in [5], LOCOSmotion can be thought of as an extension of RADAR with accelerometer-based enhancements for tracking.

Building a radio map by means of fingerprinting can be labor-intensive, hence there have been several approaches which seek to reduce the mapping effort by performing simultaneous localization and mapping [14] or using signal propagation models[12][22]. ARIADNE [12] proposes to collect only a single measurement and together with a two-dimensional construction floor plan, generates a radio map for localization. Xiang et al [22] use a signal distribution training scheme and achieve an accuracy of 5m with 90% probability for moving devices. The main limitations of indoor localization using propagation models are that due to the complexity of signal propagation in indoor environments, they either result in a high modeling effort or they only consider some of the variables affecting the signal distribution which reduces their precision.

In addition to WLAN, there are several indoor localization systems based on RFID technologies. RFID has been developed for automated identification of objects and people [13]. An RFID system usually comprises a tag and a reader. There are both active - where the tag has a battery - and passive - where the tag is induced by the reader - RFID based localization systems. LANDMARC [17] is an RFID-based localization system which uses multiple reference tags instead of multiple readers to mitigate cost. SpotON [10] is another RFID based localization system which uses custom RFID readers to detect the tag and triangulate its position using signal strength measurements. RFID systems can produce sub-meter precision levels, but have the downside of requiring extra hardware and infrastructure to be acquired and installed.

Aside from WLAN and RFID, many other RF technologies have been used for indoor localization. For example, there are IEEE 802.15.4-based [4] systems, Bluetooth-based indoor localization systems [1], Ultrawideband [11], and hybrid systems which use a combination of multiple RF technologies for indoor positioning. One such system is proposed by Baniukevic et al in [3]. It uses a combination of Bluetooth and WLAN signals for positioning. A good overview of possible approaches and technologies can be found in [15] and [7]. Most of these systems differ from LOCOSmotion in that they require extra infrastructure to be purchased which can be sometimes expensive.

3   LOCOSmotion

LOCOSmotion relies on a dense deployment of off-the-shelf wireless access points that continuously broadcast WLAN signals and provide good coverage of the target area. As with every other system that is based on RF fingerprinting, there are two phases involved in deployment; the training phase and localization phase. In the first phase – the training phase – we calibrate the system by performing WLAN scans with an Android-based mobile phone to capture and store WLAN fingerprints for several known locations. In the second phase – the localization phase – we run a background service on the mobile phone that continuously performs WLAN scans and matches the resulting fingerprint against the stored ones. The location of the closest matching fingerprint is returned as the estimated location. In between consecutive WLAN scans, accelerometer-based dead-reckoning is used to extrapolate intermediate locations using the phone's previous movement vector.

As described in [5], the LOCOSmotion system was specifically built to address the five goals set out by the EvAAL competition which are to provide a high accuracy, a low installation complexity, a high user acceptance, a high availablilty as well as enabling interoperability. In the following, we briefly explain how LOCOSmotion addresses these goals.

- *High Accuracy* – To ensure a high accuracy, LOCOSmotion relies on WLAN fingerprinting as this approach is known to exhibit better performance than systems which use simple forms of signal propagation modeling [7].
- *Low Installation Complexity* – To ensure a low installation complexity, LOCOSmotion relies on off-the-shelf hardware with customized software. To enable a speedy deployment in different environments, LOCOSmotion provides an Android application with a graphical user interface that allows the on-site collection of fingerprints for different locations.
- *High User Acceptance* – To ensure a high user acceptance, LOCOSmotion only requires the user to carry a mobile phone which performs all measurements and computations. Consequently, it is easy to integrate in the daily activities of users since many users will be already carrying a phone anyway.
- *High Availability* – Due to measurement imprecision, WLAN fingerprinting usually requires several measurements to accurately determine the location of the user. Thus, in order to achieve the location update rate goal of 2 Hz, LOCOSmotion combines fingerprinting with acceleration-based dead-reckoning.
- *Interoperability* – To enable and ease interoperability, LOCOSmotion relies solely on unmodified off-the-shelf hardware. To facilitate extensibility and to ease software integration, LOCOSmotion is using the NARF component system [8] developed by members of our research group. The NARF component system is a generic framework for personal context recognition which facilitates modularity and software reuse.

More technical details and a more thorough description of LOCOSmotion including a detailed analysis of the results of deploying and using the system during the EvAAL 2012 competition can be found in [5]. In the following sections, we focus primarily on several enhancements that we implemented and tested to improve overall performance of the system.

4   Enhancements

The LOCOSmotion system was designed to achieve a high accuracy, a low installation complexity, a high user acceptance, a high availability and interoperability. As demonstrated by the results of the EvAAL 2012 competition, the system largely fulfills the last four design goals. Yet, the results also indicate that there is considerable optimization potential with respect to installation complexity and accuracy. In the following, we discuss three enhancements to the original system that address this potential.

4.1   Training Effort

With the original implementation of LOCOSmotion, the training phase was performed by a person (the trainer) performing scans with one phone at discrete points in a grid defined on top of the target area. The scans were performed in multiple orientations to account for signal attenuation induced by the trainer. This improves accuracy, but is also time-consuming.

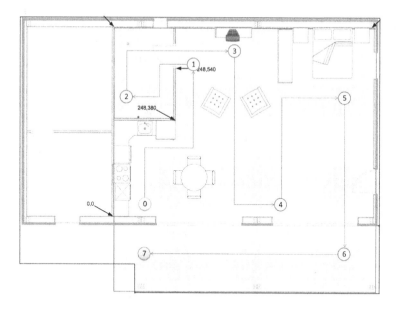

Fig. 1. Training Path and Markers

Instead of using discrete scans, we have enhanced the system to continuously perform scans while the trainer moves around. To do this, we first define a path through the area by specifying a sequence of points as shown in Figure 1. The path is chosen to maximize coverage of the areas in the building where people are likely to be found. During the training phase, the trainer then follows the path and marks his current position whenever he reaches one of the pre-defined points.

In addition, the trainer is equipped with multiple devices that are put into the left and right, front and back pockets. Multiple devices enable the coverage of different orientations to account for signal attenuation due to the human body. Taking different orientations into consideration has been shown to provide performance improvements of up to 67% [2]. In order to enable the correlation of measurements from different phones, we synchronize their clocks shortly before the training using Network Time Protocol (NTP).

Once the data collection is complete, the fingerprints from the different phones are aggregated and the (X, Y) coordinates are computed for each fingerprint by interpolating the intermediate locations based on timing information. The resulting output is a radio map with a dense distribution of the fingerprints collected from multiple devices facing different directions. Using this technique results in time savings of 75% to 83 % for training, while maintaining the accuracy of the original implementation.

4.2 Dead-reckoning

The LOCOSmotion system uses the accelerometer of the Android phone to determine its speed and extrapolate locations between WLAN scans using its previous movement vector. This enables the system to guarantee an update rate that exceeds the WLAN scanning rate. However, our original implementation used a simple algorithm that estimated the steps taken by a person by simply counting events during which the acceleration exceeded a given threshold. Despite our positive experimental laboratory evaluation, this turned out to be not very robust in the EvAAL 2012 setting as the person performing the test was following a pace-setter. This, in turn, resulted in an atypical acceleration pattern which caused imprecise intermediate estimates.

To address this issue, we completely redesigned the fundamental algorithm to determine the speed of the phone [16]. Instead of the simple threshold-based approach, the new implementation uses a tiered approach to determine the number of steps and the resulting distance covered. As a first step, we differentiate between 4 typical classes of movements, namely no movement, slow walk, normal walk and running. To do this, we determine the minimum and maximum acceleration as well as the variance over a 1 second frame using a simple tree classifier that we trained with data gathered from 5 persons. If a movement is detected, we apply a low pass filter over the signal which we parameterize with a cut-off frequency of 2, 3 or 4 Hz depending on the modality (i.e. 2 Hz for slow walking speed and 4 Hz for running). As a last step, we count the number of maximas in the frame and use this as our number of steps. Finally, in order to determine the distance covered we apply the formula described in [21]. We consistently use a k-value of 0.55 in order to avoid personalization effort.

4.3 Domotic Events

Domestic robotic (domotic) systems in home automation typically comprise automated systems that control the heating, entertainment and energy consumption and more in a home. The Living Lab in Madrid is equipped with a domotic bus which provides notifications for events in the home such as a light switch being triggered (as well as the position of the switch) and other such events. The notification typically includes the location of the triggered sensor or event.

In order to leverage this potentially valuable information, we have enhanced LOCOSmotion to enable the integration with external event providers such as a domotic bus. The provider can increase the confidence level in the location estimate or it can correct the estimate. However, we realize that in cases where multiple persons are present in the target area, purely relying on external event notifications can reduce the accuracy of the system. Thus, we only allow location corrections in cases where the distance between the estimated and the corrected location is less than the average system error. If the distance is greater than that, the external event provider is ignored.

5 Evaluation

In this section, we evaluate the performance of the enhanced LOCOSmotion system. We first look at the performance of the improved algorithm for step detection and distance estimation which forms the basis of our dead-reckoning. Then we describe the results of an experimental evaluation of the improved system in our lab and compare it to the performance of the system without any of the optimizations made in this paper. Since our laboratory is not equipped with domotic systems, we do not evaluate the potential gains, however, it should be clear that they are heavily dependent on the accuracy of the available events.

5.1 Steps and Distance Estimation

To measure the effectiveness of our improved algorithm for step detection and distance estimation, we asked three persons to walk several rounds on the parking lot in front of the university building. Each person was walking three rounds in total, each one at different speeds - representing our three movement categories (i.e. slow and normal walking and running). Before the experiment we measured the distance of a single round and during the experiment we were manually counting the steps taken by the different persons. After the experiment, we contrasted the manually counted steps with the steps determined by our algorithms. Depending on the person, the precision of the step detection stage ranged between 85 and 95%. Furthermore, we contrasted the measured distance with the computed distance which resulted in slightly lower accuracies ranging between 80 and 85%.

5.2 LOCOSmotion Localization System

The evaluation of the system was carried out on the 5th floor of our university office building. The path was traced through the pathways of the building and the passable space in the office as shown in Figure 2. So basically, every place where people are likely to be found was covered by the trainer and fingerprints were collected. One lecture hall was not covered due to its unavailability at the time of the measurements, hence no paths can be seen in in this room.

In total, we collected 1783 fingerprints from the 4 Galaxy Nexus Android mobile devices which were used by the trainer. We also collected another set of fingerprints to use for the evaluation of the system. We principally evaluate the enhancements to the system, particularly the accuracy and precision of the enhanced LOCOSmotion localization system and the time for initial calibration. Due to lack of domestic home automation infrastructure at the office building, we do not include any evaluation of the impact of considering domotic events during localization.

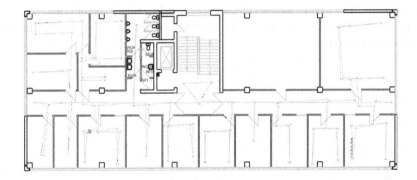

Fig. 2. Office Building Trace Path

Accuracy and Precision. The accuracy measures the average error distance of the system. The fingerprints for the evaluation were collected in the same manner as the training fingerprints, with the user walking around the office building with the mobile device. The true location of the user was again interpolated from the markers in the path and then this was compared to the location estimated by the LOCOSmotion system. Figure 3 shows the results of the evaluation.

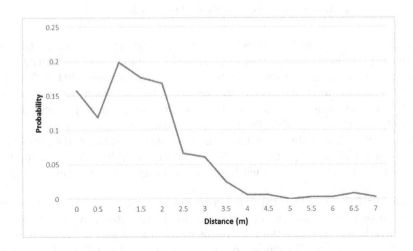

Fig. 3. Probability Distribution of Errors

The average error from the evaluation is 1.6m, the median error is 1.5m and the maximum error is 7m. The curve is a Gaussian distribution which is shifted by 1m. This is a result of the fact that for localization, we do not collect a single fingerprint for localization, but rather multiple scans are performed and smoothed and the result is used to generate a location estimate. The resulting fingerprint at each point is therefore not an absolute fingerprint at that position, but rather an aggregation of a multiple fingerprints depending on the speed at which the user is moving. We are therefore not always localizing the person where they are, but rather where they were approximately 2 seconds ago (average human walking speed is 1.4 m/s). For a user who would be running, the shift would be even greater.

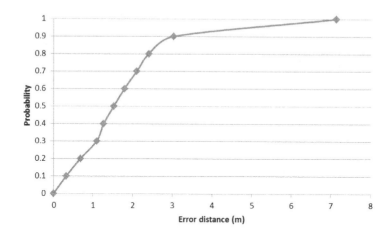

Fig. 4. Cummulative Probability Distribution of Errors

Likewise, the precision measures the success probability of location estimates with respect to the accuracy. Figure 4 shows the cumulative probability distribution of the localization system. From the figure, we can read that 60% of the location estimates have an error of 2m or less which increases to 90% at 3m. Only 10% of the values are between 3m and 7m. This is an improvement over the results from the first LOCOSmotion paper where only 34% of the time the result was within 2 neighboring cells (each of dimension 2x2m), and 83.8% of the time within 4 neighboring cells. It is obvious that the new fingerprinting method leads to dense fingerprinting which improves accuracy and precision.

Calibration Effort. The total time needed for the calibration of the entire 5th floor of our office building was 11.5 minutes. In the first iteration of LOCOSmotion, we overlaid a grid over the floor resulting in 90 locations where fingerprints were to be collected for 8 different orientations. The IEEE 802.11 standard requires that all channels be scanned during a WiFi scan. There are typically 14 WLAN channels in use and with most commercial access points broadcasting for 100ms on each channel[18], it requires a total of 1.4 seconds to perform a complete WLAN scan. Combining this with the 8 orientations and 90 points in the building, it took a total of 1.4 hours to create a complete scan of the whole floor using the previous implementation.

The new mapping system represents an over 86% reduction in (pure scanning) time required to create a fingerprint radio map. The new system also has the advantage of eliminating unnecessary points which result from a grid system and focusing on the areas and paths where people are usually found in the first place.

This leads to better coverage of the areas and faster deployment times for the LOCOSmotion system.

6   Conclusion

In this paper, we presented improvements to the LOCOSmotion indoor localization system. LOCOSmotion enables indoor localization by combining WLAN fingerprinting with speed estimations gathered from acceleration measurements and relies on standard off-the-shelf hardware which makes it very cost-efficient. The improvements proposed to the system increase its accuracy while simultaneously reducing the installation effort. Consequently, we think that it is a suitable candidate for supporting the development of many pervasive computing applications that require person tracking. At the present time, we are investigating further drive down the cost of installation and increase accuracy by making use of signal transmission properties and propagation modeling.

Acknowledgements. The research presented in this paper has been partly funded by UBICITEC and the German Federal Ministry of Education and Research as part of the WebDA project under grant number 16SV4023. The authors would like to thank Patrick Neumann for his work on LOCOSmotion's step detection components.

References

1. Akeila, E., Salcic, Z., Swain, A., Croft, A., Stott, J.: Bluetooth-based Indoor Positioning with Fuzzy based Dynamic Calibration. In: TENCON 2010 - 2010 IEEE Region 10 Conference, pp. 1415–1420 (November 2010)
2. Bahl, P., Padmanabhan, V.N.: Radar: An in-building rf-based user location and tracking system. In: IEEE Proceedings of the Nineteenth Annual Joint Conference of the IEEE Computer and Communications Societies, INFOCOM 2000, vol. 2, pp. 775–784 (2000)
3. Baniukevic, A., Sabonis, D., Jensen, C.S., Lu, H.: Improving Wi-Fi Based Indoor Positioning Using Bluetooth Add-Ons. In: 2011 IEEE 12th International Conference on Mobile Data Management, pp. 246–255 (June 2011)
4. Barsocchi, P., Lenzi, S., Chessa, S., Furfari, F.: Automatic virtual calibration of range-based indoor localization systems. Wireless Communications and Mobile Computing (12), 1546–1557 (2012)
5. Fet, N., Handte, M., Wagner, S., Marrón, P.J.: LOCOSmotion: An acceleration-assisted person tracking system based on wireless LAN. In: Chessa, S., Knauth, S. (eds.) EvAAL 2012. CCIS, vol. 362, pp. 17–31. Springer, Heidelberg (2013)
6. Focken, D., Stiefelhagen, R.: Towards vision-based 3-D people tracking in a smart room. In: Proceedings of the Fourth IEEE International Conference on Multimodal Interfaces, pp. 400–405 (2002)
7. Gu, Y., Lo, A., Niemegeers, I.: A survey of indoor positioning systems for wireless personal networks. IEEE Communications Surveys & Tutorials 11(1), 13–32 (2009)

8. Handte, M., Iqbal, U., Apolinarski, W., Wagner, S., Marrón, P.J.: The narf architecture for generic personal context recognition. In: 2010 IEEE International Conference on Sensor Networks, Ubiquitous, and Trustworthy Computing (SUTC), pp. 123–130 (June 2010)

9. Haverinen, J., Kemppainen, A.: A Global Self-localization Technique Utilizing Local Anomalies of the Ambient Magnetic Field. In: 2009 IEEE International Conference on Robotics and Automation, pp. 3142–3147 (May 2009)

10. Hightower, J., Want, R., Borriello, G.: SpotON: An indoor 3D location sensing technology based on RF signal strength. UW CSE 00-02-02, University of Washington (2000)

11. Ingram, S.J., Harmer, D., Quinlan, M.: Ultrawideband indoor positioning systems and their use in emergencies. In: Position Location and Navigation Symposium, PLANS 2004, pp. 706–715 (2004)

12. Ji, Y., Biaz, S., Pandey, S., Agrawal, P.: Ariadne: A dynamic indoor signal map construction and localization system. In: Proceedings of the 4th International Conference on Mobile Systems, Applications and Services, MobiSys 2006, pp. 151–164. ACM, New York (2006)

13. Juels, A.: RFID Security and Privacy: A Research Survey. IEEE Journal on Selected Areas in Communications 24(2), 381–394 (2006)

14. Lim, H., Kung, L.-C., Hou, J.C., Luo, H.: Zero-configuration indoor localization over ieee 802.11 wireless infrastructure. Wireless Networks 16(2), 405–420 (2010)

15. Liu, H., Darabi, H., Banerjee, P., Liu, J.: Survey of wireless indoor positioning techniques and systems. IEEE Transactions on Systems, Man, and Cybernetics, Part C: Applications and Reviews 37(6), 1067–1080 (2007)

16. Neumann, P.: A system for inertia-based distance estimation using mobile phones. University of Duisburg-Essen, Bachelor Thesis (July 2012)

17. Ni, L.M., Liu, Y., Lau, Y.C., Patil, A.P.: Landmarc: Indoor location sensing using active rfid. Wireless Networks 10, 701–710 (2004), doi:10.1023/B:WINE.0000044029.06344.dd

18. Velayos, H., Karlsson, G.: Techniques to reduce the ieee 802.11b handoff time. In: 2004 IEEE International Conference on Communications, vol. 7, pp. 3844–3848 (2004)

19. Want, R., Hopper, A., Falcão, V., Gibbons, J.: The Active Badge Location System. ACM Transactions on Information Systems 10(1), 91–102 (1992)

20. Ward, A., Jones, A., Hopper, A.: A new location technique for the active office. IEEE Personal Communications 4(5), 42–47 (1997)

21. Weinberg, H.: Using the adxl202 in pedometer and personal navigation applications. iMEMS Technologies/Applications, Analog Devices (1995)

22. Xiang, Z., Song, S., Chen, J., Wang, H., Huang, J., Gao, X.: A wireless lan-based indoor positioning technology. IBM Journal of Research and Development 48(5.6), 617–626 (2004)

AmbiTrack - Marker-free Indoor Localization and Tracking of Multiple Users in Smart Environments with a Camera-based Approach

Andreas Braun[1] and Tim Dutz[2]

[1] Fraunhofer Institute for Computer Graphics Research IGD, Darmstadt, Germany
andreas.braun@igd.fraunhofer.de
[2] TU Darmstadt, KOM - Multimedia Communications Lab, Darmstadt, Germany
tim.dutz@kom.tu-darmstadt.de

Abstract. Systems providing tracking and localization of persons in an indoor environment have been continuously proposed in recent years, particularly for Pervasive Computing applications. AmbiTrack is a system that provides marker-free localization and tracking, i.e., it does not require the users to carry any tag with them in order to perform localization. This allows easy application in circumstances where wearing a tag is not viable, e.g. in typical Ambient Assisted Living scenarios, where users may not be well-versed technologically. In this work, we present the AmbiTrack system and its adaptation for the EvAAL competition 2013. We present a marker-free, camera-based system for usage in indoor environments designed for cost-effectiveness and reliability. We adapt our previously presented system to make it more reliable in tracking multiple persons, using context information for improving recognition rate and simplifying the installation.

Keywords: Indoor localization, Computer Vision, Ambient Assisted Living.

1 Introduction

The reliable localization and tracking of various users is one of the main challenges in the research area of smart environments. The knowledge of the users' position is a core contextual information for assistive systems that need to decide in periodic intervals, whether or not they are supposed to influence the actual state of their environment via one or multiple of their actuators available. While basic motion sensors are in many cases able to deliver sufficient information when one person is concerned, the tracking of multiple persons typically requires more sophisticated solutions. This is equally important when the system needs to distinguish between users and non-critical actors in the environment, such as pets.

Various indoor tracking and localization approaches for usage in conjunction with Ambient Intelligence systems have been proposed and there are even specific competitions with the intention of comparing the different methods' performances against one another [1]. Three different categories of localization methods can be distinguished, active marker-based solutions, passive marker-based solutions, and

J.A. Botía et al. (Eds.): EvAAL 2013, CCIS 386, pp. 83–93, 2013.
© Springer-Verlag Berlin Heidelberg 2013

marker-free solutions. Both active and passive marker-based solutions require a person to carry some type of tag in order to enable localization. A multitude of reasons make these types of solutions less favorable, such as higher cost and a user's tendency to forget the tags. Marker-free solutions are capable of localizing persons independently of whether they are carrying additional accessories. Examples for approaches from this latter category include capacitive sensitive floors [2], using microphones for the detection of subtle noises caused by movement [3], and camera-based approaches [4]. The three main criteria that all of these localization solutions are judged on are the total costs for providing them for a specific area, such as a private apartment, their reliability, and the amount of persons that can be tracked and distinguished by them at a time.

In this work, we present AmbiTrack, a marker-free, camera-based approach for use in typical indoor environments, which allows the reliable localization of multiple persons. For EvAAL we are building upon a previously presented system that was able to successfully track two users in parallel [5]. This paper will present the findings of this previous publication in a partially shortened form and also present the adaptations made as relevant for the EvAAL competition in detail.

2   Related Work

Detecting the presence and location of persons has been a research effort for many decades and as such, can now be achieved using a variety of technologies. Capacitive sensors use oscillating electric fields to measure the properties of an electric field and so allow the detection of a human body's presence. Braun et al. have presented a system using electrodes laid out in a grid and hidden underneath the floor covering to detect the location of one or more persons [2]. A similar system that integrates necessary electronics into a floor layer and which communicates wirelessly with a central system has been presented by Lauterbach et al. [6]. Both systems furthermore allow the realization of additional use cases, such as intrusion detection.

Walking is creating a certain level of noise that can be picked up by microphones and used to infer the location of persons. Most of the systems based on this concept use time-of-flight techniques; that is, calculating the distance of the source by measuring the time required for the signal to arrive at a specific location and triangulating its position [3]. While earlier system relied on speech to recognize sound sources [7], newer and more sensitive systems allow the detection of a person from the sound of her footsteps [8].

Another popular method (that requires an active token to be worn) is based on different radio frequency techniques, e.g., by measuring signal strength (RSSI) on different receivers and triangulate the positions [9]. A newer approach is using tomography techniques to measure the signal attenuation by human bodies [10] and allows a localization without requiring a person to wear active tokens.

Finally, the method that our work is based on comes from the area of computer vision and uses different types of cameras [11], depending on visible light or infrared depth imaging [12]. Most systems use similar approaches that use background subtraction to detect movement in single images or time-series of images to infer the position of an object [4].

3   System Design

The following section describes the design decisions that have been driving the development of our AmbiTrack system, whereby the main requirement was to provide a cost-efficient solution that nonetheless achieves a high reliability. The resulting effects on hardware architecture and software platform are outlined on the next pages.

3.1   System Requirements

The system is based on a set of standard, off-the-shelf webcams and as such excels through its low cost factor – the hardware cost for an average living room should be less than 100 $ (provided that a PC is already available). There are three main challenges associated to the design of such a system for smart environments:

- Scalability - it should be easy to attach additional cameras to the system and provide tools that allow setting the position and orientation of the video devices within the environment
- Flexibility - the system should be able to distinguish between different persons and discard other moving objects, such as pets
- Computational Feasibility - the algorithms used for person localization should be suitable for usage with low-resolution, low-bandwidth data, while still being able to reliably recognize moving persons
- Abstraction - the algorithms and hardware should allow for future implementation in privacy-preserving smart camera systems

The system we are using is set up using a simple configuration tool that models the environment and the extrinsic camera parameters by way of XML files. The video stream of each camera is analyzed for signs of movement and we register the results of each camera to the others. This allows the generation of three-dimensional data of moving objects and the inference of such an object's position within the environment. At least two cameras must capture the moving object for the method to work. In border cases, we use approximations and historical movement data to estimate the object's position. We are using simple metrics to distinguish between different persons, based on the color of their clothing and body volume.

3.2   Hardware Architecture

The system is comprised of various nodes made up of a single PC with various USB cameras attached. They are connected to each other using either a wired LAN connection (preferably), or WiFi. The cameras used should be controllable in terms of

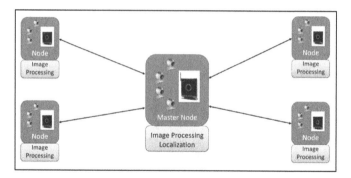

Fig. 1. Hardware architecture of the localization system

modifying their settings, such as automatic settings of white balance, gain, contrast and brightness. This allows offloading the image processing to the individual nodes, and in consequence only higher-level features are sent through the network connections. This is reducing the required bandwidth and makes this approach feasible for low-speed wireless networks. One of the nodes is acting as a master, analyzes the high-level data and provides the overall processing of the final localization. The overall architecture is shown in Figure 1.

3.3   Data Processing

Our system is following a regular camera-based indoor localization process, as shown in Figure 2. Each individual system is processing the image of the camera using a motion detection algorithm. We use a custom variant of background subtraction that allows a fine-grained control of the sample window, camera parameters and feature size, thus guaranteeing swift adaptation to different room geometries. In a second step, we extract features from the detected motion, in our case the center of gravity of each moving region and metrics about the detected regions, which allow us to identify individual persons in a future iteration. Only these features (and not the entire stream) are then being sent over the network for further processing. Finally, the master system is collecting all the features, combines it with its local representation of the environment and performs the actual localization of the different persons.

Fig. 2. Localization process

We have implemented a controlling software which realizes all these steps and also provides various tools to support the entire AmbiTrack system setup and maintenance process. These tools include:

- Camera management: add/remove cameras, set intrinsic and extrinsic parameters
- Environment management: read layout from image files
- Camera placement tools: coverage analysis, coverage optimization
- Performance analysis: show CPU load, network status, logging

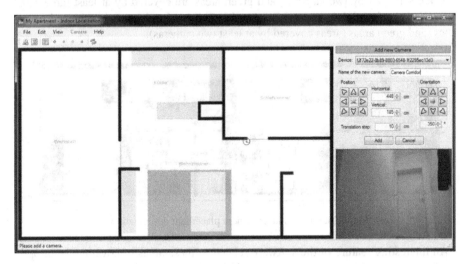

Fig. 3. Software's main view

Figure 3 shows a screenshot of the software's main user interface. On the left, we can see the source image file of the environment. Using a threshold-based processing, the boundaries are extracted from the black areas indicating walls. On the right side of the figure, we can see the wizard that allows the adding of additional cameras.

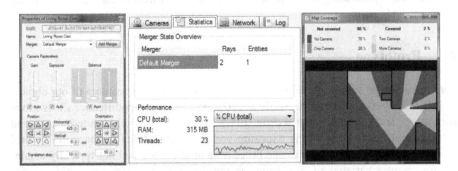

Fig. 4. Camera properties (left), Statistics (center), Coverage analysis (right)

The wizards of the software enable us to modify the position and orientation of cameras and check on the live camera stream. Once a camera is added, it is also possible to control the results of the image processing in a dedicated window and individually set post-processing parameters, such as white balance and color correction (Figure 4 - left). The statistics window, as shown on Figure 4 (center), gives an overview of the available master nodes (mergers) and the load on all available CPU cores, as well as the number of currently active threads. Finally, the coverage map shown on Figure 4 (right) displays by color, which areas of the environment are currently covered by cameras, and by how many (red indicates blind spots, orange areas are in the view of a single camera, yellow areas are surveyed by two cameras, and green areas are covered by at least three cameras). We have found that, as a rule of thumb, a reliable localization is achieved for all yellow and green areas (areas covered by at least two cameras).

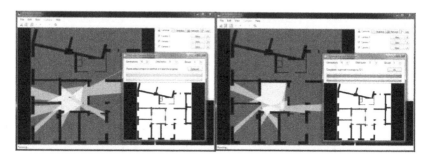

Fig. 5. Before and after camera placement optimization

An interesting feature of the software related to these areas of coverage is an optimization algorithm for camera placement. Using the camera coverage area as a quality metric, a genetic algorithm is used to calculate optimal camera positioning. The algorithm optimizes camera placement based on the number of available cameras and considers wall and ceiling positions as an additional restriction (Figure 5).

The software was created using C# and the .NET runtime environment. For image processing, we are using EmguCV[1], a .NET wrapper for OpenCV[2]. This is a comprehensive image processing and computer vision library, which already provides many of the methods required.

4   Prototype

For our prototype set-up, we selected the Playstation Eye as the camera of our choice, as it is available at a low price, while nevertheless allowing modifications to various parameters, such as frames per second (FPS), deactivation of auto-white-balance and auto-contrast, as well as setting exposure and gain. The ability to manually control these parameters is crucial for image processing applications and not typically available for cheaper varieties of web cams. While the system is easily scalable, for our initial tests we have used only two nodes, with two cameras attached to each of those (which results in a total of four cameras). This setup has proven to be sufficient for covering a fairly large room (roughly 35 square meters). Both nodes were running our

---

[1] http://www.emgu.com
[2] http://opencv.org/

Fig. 6. Playstation Eye camera out-of-the-box

software on 64-bit multi-core processors (AMD Turion 64 and Intel Core i5). The cameras are running at 30 FPS and VGA resolution (640x480). The CPU load and amounts of threads used indicate that each node would be able to handle at least twice the number of cameras. RAM requirements have generally shown to be low and as not being the limiting factor.

The system was installed in our institute's Living Lab, which consists of a combined living room and kitchen area, a bedroom and an office. For our evaluation, only the combined living room and kitchen area were considered. The combined area covered is approximately 35 square meters and is occupied by several large pieces of furniture (cupboards, desks, and the like). Therefore, a sophisticated camera placement is crucial in order to guarantee a good coverage. The software tools as described previously were essential for finding optimal camera positions in this setting. As a next logical step, we intend to extend our prototype setup to all rooms of the Living Lab.

5   Evaluation

As indicated before, we have been able to successfully test our prototype system (software and hardware setup) for the simultaneous tracking of two persons, using four cameras to cover an above average-sized room. By using the camera placement optimization algorithm, we positioned the four cameras on different corners of the room and thus maximized the area covered by at least three devices. The screenshot one can see on Figure 7 shows the software's main screen with the apartment's map on the left and one camera's viewing angle highlighted. The image stream of this selected camera can be seen on the lower right. The frame on the upper right shows the persons that are currently tracked by this camera (supported by the feeds delivered by the other three cameras). Making use of small markers on the floor, we have been able to verify that our system's distance estimation feature is actually very precise for

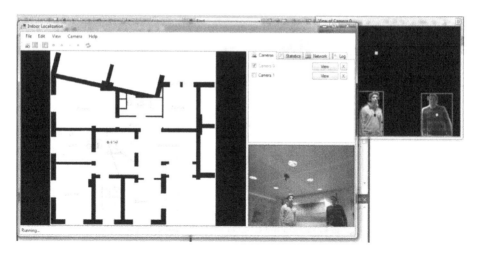

Fig. 7. The simultaneous detection of two persons

areas that are covered by at least three cameras (the estimation was rarely more than 30 cm off the mark). The processing power of the two medium-class PCs we used for handling the four camera's image streams proved to be more than capable for this and showed significant reserves. Based on this, we intend to investigate two potential options. First, to build a new prototype system which will use only a single PC for handling four, six, or maybe even eight cameras at once and which could then be used to monitor an entire small apartment and second, to make use of efficient smart cameras that are capable of entirely processing a single camera stream, thus significantly reducing the network overhead and also providing a higher perceived privacy (through reducing the amount of shared data).

6   AmbiTrack @ EvAAL

Our system had to undergo some modifications in order to qualify as a contender for the EvAAL Competition for Indoor Localization 2013. Some of these have already been described, but will also be detailed in this section.

One major challenge of EvAAL is the installation time measurement. This requires the system to be set up swiftly and by as few persons as possible. Regarding camera-based systems, it is important that both position and orientation of a device are easily configurable and can be reproduced on location. Therefore, we have taken several measures to improve the installation and configuration of AmbiTrack.

The first improvement allows the easy import of floor plans into the software. The user can select any floor plan image file and AmbiTrack will analyze the image contents to detect walls. This allows easily creating configured floor plans from created images without requiring XML configuration by hand. The process is shown on

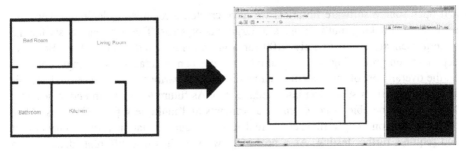

Fig. 8. Import of floor plans into AmbiTrack software

Figure 8. The image processing algorithm is looking for a certain brightness level to find walls and cuts of brighter parts of the images, such as the descriptive text on the map on the left side of the Figure. Currently each pixel is associated to a distance of 1 cm. In future iterations we plan on allowing a more flexible configuration of pixel-to-distance conversion.

Fig. 9. Custom built stand for Playstation Eye camera

Additionally, we have designed a custom stand that allows the easy attachment of the cameras on walls, as shown in Figure 9. It is a simple wooden structure that allows the attachment of a single camera. Additionally the orientation of the camera can be controlled by attached scales. The camera stand can be attached to both walls and ceilings and thus provides a high amount of flexibility. The goal is to easily recreate the configuration on the actual location that has been configured in the software.

7   Conclusion and Future Work

On the previous pages we have presented AmbiTrack, a system for localizing and tracking multiple persons indoor. Built entirely from affordable, off-the-shelf hardware and open source software libraries, we have created a reliable, scalable and versatile solution for tracking multiple users in large indoor areas. The hardware costs for the system itself are approximately $100 for four cameras, stands and cabling. Because, depending on processing power, multiple cameras can be attached to a single computer, the overall cost of the system remains low even if various cameras are used. Ambi-Track in its current state is an intermediate step. As future work, we intend to scale up the system to be able to cover entire apartments and multiple separated rooms. Also, the identification of specific users as realized in its current state is rudimentary at best and requires further testing. As a next step, we will thus test different identification features and investigate, how many persons the system can be reliably differentiate. In terms of hardware, we would like to evaluate different types of cameras, such as the Microsoft Kinect for depth imaging, which should allow for a more reliable background subtraction and thus is potentially better suited for scenarios where many users are present. Finally, we would also like to test self-organizing networks for smart cameras that perform image processing on an included chip and send features to each other using wireless communication systems. Self-localization and registration are further aspects we would like to explore in this regard.

Acknowledgements. We would like to thank Michael Alekseew and Philipp Schillinger from the Technische Universität Darmstadt for their major contributions in our efforts of creating the AmbiTrack system.

References

1. Chessa, S., Knauth, S. (eds.): EvAAL 2011. CCIS, vol. 309, pp. 14–25. Springer, Heidelberg (2012)
2. Braun, A., Heggen, H., Wichert, R.: CapFloor – A Flexible Capacitive Indoor Localization System. In: Chessa, S., Knauth, S. (eds.) EvAAL 2011. CCIS, vol. 309, pp. 26–35. Springer, Heidelberg (2012)
3. Brandstein, M.S., Silverman, H.F.: A practical methodology for speech source localization with microphone arrays. Computer Speech Language 11, 91–126 (1997)
4. Krumm, J., Harris, S., Meyers, B., Brumitt, B., Hale, M., Shafer, S.: Multi-camera multi-person tracking for EasyLiving. In: Proceedings of the Third IEEE International Workshop on Visual Surveillance, pp. 3–10. IEEE Comput. Soc. (2000)
5. Braun, A., Dutz, T., Alekseew, M., Schillinger, P., Marinc, A.: Marker-Free Indoor Localization and Tracking of Multiple Users in Smart Environments Using a Camera-Based Approach. In: Streitz, N., Stephanidis, C. (eds.) DAPI 2013. LNCS, vol. 8028, pp. 349–357. Springer, Heidelberg (2013)
6. Lauterbach, C., Steinhage, A.: SensFloor ® - A Large-area Sensor System Based on Printed Textiles Printed Electronics. In: Ambient Assisted Living Congress. VDE Verlag (2009)
7. Sturim, D., Silverman, H., Brandstein, M.: Tracking Multiple Talkers Using Microphone-Array Measurements. In: Proceedings of the 1997 IEEE International Conference on Acoustics, Speech, and Signal Processing, ICASSP 1997, p. 371 (1997)
8. Guo, Y., Hazas, M.: Localising speech, footsteps and other sounds using resource-constrained devices. In: 2011 10th International Conference on Information Processing in Sensor Networks (IPSN), pp. 330–341 (2011)

9. Balakrishnan, H.: The Cricket Indoor Location System, Dissertation, Massachusetts Institute of Technology (2005)
10. Wilson, J., Patwari, N.: See-Through Walls: Motion Tracking Using Variance-Based Radio Tomography Networks. IEEE Transactions on Mobile Computing 10, 612–621 (2011)
11. de Ipiña, D.L.: TRIP: A low-cost vision-based location system for ubiquitous computing. Personal and Ubiquitous Computing 6, 206–219 (2002)
12. Shotton, J., Fitzgibbon, A., Cook, M., Sharp, T., Finocchio, M., Moore, R., Kipman, A., Blake, A.: Real-time human pose recognition in parts from single depth images. Communications of the ACM 56, 116–124 (2013)

Mobile Robot Platform to track User Movement and Behaviour

Melvin Isken, Bjoern Borgmann, and Andreas Hein

OFFIS e.V., Escherweg 2, 26121 Oldenburg
melvin.isken@offis.de
http://www.offis.de

Abstract. This document describes a currently developed robotic system that tracks and analyses human gait parameters. This system is used to conduct mobility assessments to track the user's health status. Mobility assessments conducted by a mobile robot provide significant advantages over current methodologies. Additionally, the robot navigation capabilities can be enhanced by the use of mobility assessment data. Parts of the overall concept are evaluated by the evAAL competition 2013, Track 1, Indoor Localization and Tracking.

Keywords: mobile robot, mobility assessment, laser range finder.

1 Introduction

The demographic change will cause various challenges to the society within the next years. Along with an ageing society age-related medical conditions will pose a growing problem. Without a large number of younger people forming the financial base or filling the role of caregivers, the health care systems will have to cope with major logistical and economical challenges. The individual care time available per person will decrease when less caregiver face a growing number of clients. Even nowadays the time spent per client is reduced to a minimum due to economical factors. Consequential the care system has to adapt to the changing situation. One tool to ease the caregivers and their clients lives is the use of assistive technologies [1]. These technologies are not used to replace personal care but to release caregivers of collateral tasks that take concentration off of the client. Assistive technologies can be used in various areas of personal care as well as personal assistance. Typical deployment fields are work, daily living and personal as well as professional care. They can assist in prevention, stationary/ambulant treatment and rehabilitation. This will both unload the caregiver and reduce costs. Concepts like smart environments integrate components in domestic environments providing special services. Their actuators and sensors can provide service features to the residents as well as they can be used to record health related data. However, upgrading existing residences with sensors and actuators might be costly. In contrast, service robots can be easily integrated in homes carrying a set of sensors and actuators. They are intended to play an important role helping to manage the demand of caregivers by assisting elderly in

J.A. Botía et al. (Eds.): EvAAL 2013, CCIS 386, pp. 94–105, 2013.

their daily life [2]. Instead of static components with limited point of views and ranges, a mobile platform provides services in-place and simultaneously gathers information. With further developments mobile robotic platforms designed for elderly may be available as "off the shelf" products. Such upcoming technologies can be used to implement long-term monitoring of residents.

The approach presented here is a service that will enable mobility assessments using a robot. Mobility is an important factor regarding the health status of older adults. Measuring mobility can help recognizing early signs of mental decline as well as the risk of falls.

2   Medical Motivation

Environment Factor. If people are not able to cope with daily life activities by themselves they need professional care that supports them. In most cases people want to stay at home as long as possible. Moving people to a hospital or similar facility causes a strong decline in their personal feeling of healthiness. Furthermore, elderly people have their own habits and their own speed of life. Bringing them to a highly optimized and scheduled environment like a hospital, they can't keep pace with the changed surroundings. That often leads to a further and steeper decline of the health status. So the goal is to keep them in their known environments.

Mobility. A key factor for perceived quality of life is a person's mobility. From a medical perspective, being able to move around and to keep up certain body positions is a fundamental requirement for an independent lifestyle [3]. Mobility normally changes during age. Starting at the age of 60 years, elderly peoples' mobility characteristics change [4] i.e. self-selected gait velocity decreases each decade by 12%-16% during self-imposed activities. The decrease is often caused by a reduced step length whereas the step frequency remains stable.

Benefits of Long-Term Mobility Assessments. Two of the major factors influencing the proportionally higher costs to the health care system caused by elderly people are the costs due to the high need of care of demented people [5] and fall-related costs. From a clinical perspective, long-term monitoring of changes in mobility has a high potential for early diagnosis of various diseases. Therefore there is a demand for assessments to determine the risk to fall [6]. This may help delaying need of care or preventing acute incidents like falls and may thus help saving costs. On a more personal level early detection may help supporting an independent lifestyle by enabling early and purposeful prevention and may therefore increase quality of life for affected people, relatives, and care givers.

3   Related Work

3.1   Mobility Trend Analysis in Domestic Environments

Environments equipped with various sensors especially from the home automation or security domain are referred to as (health) smart homes [7]. Only some systems which use ambient sensors for detailed mobility analysis have been described so far. The research focus is on general mobility trend analysis instead. Various groups use home automation technologies like motion sensors, light barriers or reed contacts placed in door frames or on the ceiling. Cameron et al. [8] presented a solution with optical and ultrasonic sensors. These were placed in door frames to determine the walking speed and direction of a person passing. Kaye et al. [9] presented study based on sensors covering different rooms of a flat. The use of more precise sensors i.e. laser range finders (LRF) have been applied to implement very precise gait analysis in domestic environments. An approach presented by Pallejà et al. [10]. The advantage of this approach is the very detailed analysis, but it has some requirements. The person has to walk straightly towards the scanner and on a predefined path. In our own work using LRF [3] we do not restrict a person's walking path while measuring. This approach is highly precise and does not require any predefined knowledge but is more expensive to implement compared to the approach using home automation technology.

3.2   Precise Gait Analysis

Laboratory equipment for mobility monitoring provides the most precise measurements of mobility so far. Examples of such equipment are marker-based camera systems or fluoroscopy systems for cinematic gait analysis (overview in [11]). Nevertheless, the equipment is too large or complicated for being applied outside of a large laboratory and can only be handled by experts. Some systems require the patient to perform difficult calibration tasks which are not suitable for cognitive impaired or elderly people [12].

Body worn sensors reduce the need of external equipment and can provide precise analysis of gait parameters. For example, Zijlstra [13] or Aminian [14] use gyroscopes attached to the body to measure gait parameters. Another approach is to use 'electronic textiles', like Liu [15] did. Those approaches reduce the number of external sensors but require the user to actively put on and wear such devices.

Recently, LRF (previously e.g. applied in robot navigation and pedestrian detection systems for cars) have first been used in the domain of gait analysis. Pallejà et al. [10] utilize such a device to determine the length of stance and swing phase within each gait cycle and then compute the additional gait parameters average step width and average body speed. However, applicability of the approach is limited by requiring people to walk straightly towards the scanning device during the measurements. Both feet have to be kept on separate sides of drawn line which will be very difficult to apply in domestic environments and especially with mobility-impaired or elderly people. Frenken et al. [16] have integrated a LRF into a geriatric assessment tool to be used in hospital setups as well as domestic environments.

3.3   Service Robotics

Service robots combine results of different fields of robotic research into systems that are specifically targeted at an application. As technology advances, more fields of application will be made accessible. For health care robotics research started with fixed workstations [17], going over wheelchair mounted systems and intelligent wheelchairs [18], to autonomous mobile robot systems [19]. Today there are multiple mobile robots for health assistance available (commercially or for research purposes). Such systems like Robocare [20] or Care-O-bot [19] deal with helping, guiding, and assisting people at home. Most of these platforms are still in (advanced) research states. Recently, tele-presence robots and mobile transportation robots are deployed in hospital environments, like the RP-7i (www.intouchhealth.com). The limiting factor despite technical challenges is the currently high costs for such systems.

3.4   Limitation of the State of the Art

Within the domain of health care and rehabilitation service robotics there are quite few systems commercially available. Further, there is no robotic system that is capable of doing mobility assessments and tries to learn from such data for optimal observation and robotic path planning. Most of the systems are in research states. This leads to a comparably high price as well as designs that are not feasible for daily home usage (bulky, can move only on flat floor etc.). Acceptance of robots in terms of direct human-robot interaction is heavily examined currently. Most of the domestic monitoring systems providing data about mobility by use of ambient sensors do not continuously observe the person concerned (in terms of following the person). Only presence at specific known points is measured. Thus this kind of monitoring is measuring mobility indirectly and can therefore only analyse trends instead of a precise assessment to determine the mobility of a person. Laboratory equipment for precise assessments of the mobility is too large or complicated for being applied in domestic homes. It is often bound to a specific place due to the large setup and difficult to use for the non-professional. Body worn sensors require the user to actively wear them and make him aware of the 'observation situation' like putting on a blood pressure meter. In summary there is currently no system or approach available that is capable of doing precise, unobtrusive and continuous mobility assessments in domestic environments and that is additionally learning from the user's behaviour (movement) to get optimal assessment results.

4   Approach

The approach presented here is the development of a mobile robot platform capable of doing mobility assessments in domestic environments. The user tracking algorithm which is developed is explained in the next sections. At the current state of development, the system is based on a single LRF sensor. This means

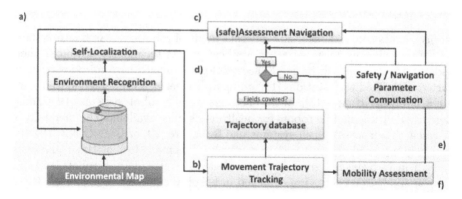

Fig. 1. Concept scheme

that no complete mobility assessment can be observed currently. The sensor is able to track peoples legs and movement of legs but no further details like movement of joints or the whole body. That means that single gait parameters are measured. We consider user tracking with a wide angle long distance sensor like a LRF as base for unobtrusive monitoring. The Kinect sensor has a narrow field of view and though requires a lot of re-positioning of the robot, which can be very annoying during daily activities. Therefore we first concentrate on getting as much useful information out of the LRF data as possible. The next step is to integrate 3D data to enable complete mobility assessments.

Concept

The method used to analyse the user's movement and adapt the navigation behaviour can be broken down into six steps (Figure 1).

Exploration and Mapping of the Environment (a). Before any navigation and further functionality can take place, the environment needs to get explored and mapped. This should be done automatically since the goal is to deploy this system without the need of extra administration effort. SLAM (self localization and mapping) strategies have been heavily investigated during the past years and research is still going on. State of the art algorithms are used in this context, no further research has been done. Enhancements like semantic mapping would increase the performance of the overall system but are not integrated / tested so far.

Track the User's Walking Paths (b). Getting information of the user's movement paths by analysing LRF data is of major interest for this process. This provides information of which areas in the environment are frequently used and where the user doesn't stay. This information is used by the following steps of the procedure.

Navigate Using the Information of the User's Paths (c). When information about frequently used paths is available, the robot is able to take them into account for its own navigation behaviour. For example, the robot should not stop in middle of a walking path where it becomes a dangerous obstacle.

Recognize and Rate Best Observation Places (d). In order to optimize the mobility assessments, the robot should find places where the observation range is maximized. This could be a spot next to a corridor where a long straight walking path is available or a spot between the couch and the TV which is walked regularly.

Determination of Safe Places, Paths and Avoiding Strategies (e). Beneath finding the best observation places, the robot should care that those places do not endanger the user additionally. The robot should select places that are as unobtrusive as possible, do not disturb the user and do not risk becoming an obstacle (optimal observation lots, OOLs). If there is an encounter between robot and user, the robot should have evading strategies that bring the robot out of the user's travel paths.

Execution of (long term, unobtrusive) Mobility Assessments (f). By using all these strategies the robot should act as unobtrusive monitoring system that is capable of assessing the mobility of the user over long periods of time. During this time the robot is able to adapt to the user's behaviour and re-select optimal observation positions.

5   Implementation

The implementation is based on a TurtleBot platform developed by Willow Garage (www.turtlebot.com) which is equipped with a laser range finder Hokuyo URG-04LX and a Microsoft Kinect sensor. Two control PCs are used, both are running Ubuntu 12.04 operating system and the robot control logic is using the ROS framework [21]. Software components are developed in C++ and Python code. The robot is depicted in (Figure 5 (a)).

5.1   User Tracking

Person Recognition. The person recognition consists of three different steps to identify a person (in terms of recognizing a person within the LRF data). All these have to be done dynamically since the robot can be moving during recognition. The first step is the background subtraction. The background is filtered out and only measurements that belong to moving objects remain. The next step is called segmentation where the measurements are grouped into objects. These objects are filtered depending on their size. Finally objects within a certain radius are classified as a person.

Background Subtraction. This component filters the static objects that belong to walls or tables. Usually this is done by using a histogram for the measurements of the LRF, but since the robot and therefore the LRF is moving this is not possible. To overcome this issue all measurements are converted into Cartesian coordinates. A map of the environment is used as a reference. Using this method all

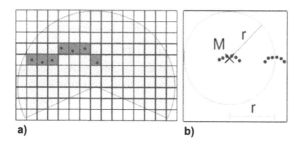

Fig. 2. a) LRF and detected objects marked as static in the occupancy grid; b) Definition of leg segments belonging to a person: two 'legs' are within distance r

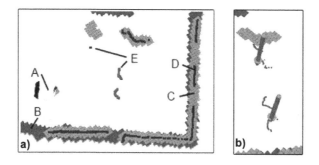

Fig. 3. a) Map after background substraction. A: robot position, B: wall (provided by map), C: marked static fields, D: (black dots) current LRF data, E: moving objects (black dots outside of static fields); b) Two persons detected within a scene, marked by an arrow.

detected objects will keep their position regardless of the movement of the robot. However, due to sensor noise and the movement of the robot, it is very difficult to detect the exact same spot again on the same accuracy level as a static LRF could do. The static LRF has an accuracy of roughly 1 cm, the dynamic algorithm takes a 5x5 cm grid for regarding measurements as static objects.

Figure 2 (a) shows an example of such a grid. The grey area is the field of view of the LRF. The black dots illustrate the actual measurements. All detected fields are marked with a dark grey. This indicates that a static object was found in this field.

Figure 3 (a) shows the result of this process. In this case two human legs can be observed (not known at this time). The current LRF measurements (D) are used to identify moving objects. Static objects are marked in a grid (C). Fields that have been occupied after the initial static grid map has been created are considered as moving objects (E).

Segmentation. This component only considers measurements that belong to moving objects since only those should contain the measurements of a moving human. The LRF is mounted on the robot in the height of human tibia (25 cm),

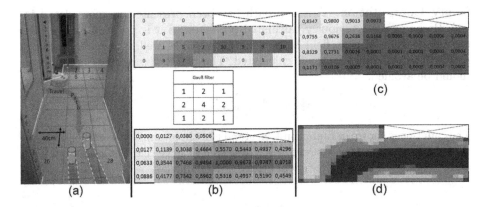

Fig. 4. Computation of safety parameters of floor segments

so all objects are filtered by their dimension. Objects that are to small or too big to form a human leg are discarded. The actual size can be software defined. The output should only contain objects with the size of human legs.

Clustering. After all segments are extracted persons can be detected. All segments should have a suitable dimension, but in order to assure that the segments really belong to a leg, a certain region around each segment is checked for another extracted segment (Figure 2 (b)). Normally a radius of 0.5 m was used, which is the maximum distance between the middle of each segment. In case two segments are found, the center of the two segments is determined as the position of the person. This way it is also possible to detect several persons. The screen shot (Figure 3 (b)) shows two arrows that indicate the positions of two persons. The dots are measurements of human legs.

Movement Analysis. This component monitors the positions of the detected persons and monitors the movement. That information is analysed and compared to a map of the home to determine regularly used paths and rarely used spots. This data is processed to calculate the safety of rarely used spots in order to find qualified spots that can be used to stay and observe the person without endangering the human.

Movement Computation. At first the path of the person is monitored. Every position which was used by the person is marked. Similar to the grid described for LRF data another grid is used to store this information. Each field contains the number of uses. One field is approximately as big as the robot (Figure 4 (a)) (can be tuned to other sizes if necessary). Every time a person enters a field the count value of that field is incremented (Figure 4 (b) top). Not all unused fields are equally qualified. If the robot is positioned on an unused field next to an often used field it can quickly become an obstacle. In order to take this into account a Gaussian filter is used and the results are normalized between 0 and 1 (Figure 4 (b) middle and bottom).

Safety Computation. This approach has been presented in more detail in [22]. Based on the previously calculated probabilities it is possible to generate the safety value of each field by considering walls as well as neighbour fields. At first the avoidance factor is calculated. The bigger the number the more it should be avoided.

$$f_a = \frac{1}{n_i} \sum_{j=0}^{n_i} r_j \tag{1}$$

The equation is shown in Equation 1. n_i stands for the amount of cross-neighbours, while i is the index of the current field. j is the index of the current neighbour field and r_j equals the probability of that field.

$$f_s = \frac{1}{k_i} \left(\sum_{k=0}^{k_i} (1 - r_k) \right)^2 \tag{2}$$

In addition the avoidance factor a stumbling factor is calculated in order to classify the risk value of a field (Equation 2). In this equation k_i stands for the amount of all existing neighbours. In both equations walls are not counted. Fields at the edge of the grid have fewer neighbours than fields in the middle. r_k is the current probability of the neighbour k. The complete formula can be seen in Equation 3. The result is a value between 0 and 1 and equals the safety of the current field. The higher the value the better the safety.

$$S_i = \frac{1}{1 + e^{\tanh(r_i + f_a - f_s)}} \tag{3}$$

The result can be seen in Figure 4 (c). Often used fields are rated bad (dark color). The safety of a neighbour field is rated good (bright color) as long as there is enough space for the robot to avoid an approaching human. Figure 4 (d) shows such a grid in a higher resolution (fields are smaller than the actual robot size).

Analysis. An analysis of the tracked persons is performed while the persons are observed. Mainly the average walking speed and the walking direction is calculated. This is done by using the position of the detected persons and the time between the detection. Figure 5 (b) shows a walking person. The line of dots indicates the positions in which the person was recognized. The arrow shows the current direction of the person. The five latest positions are used to calculate the average velocity and the direction.

Person Observation. In order to achieve a continuous observation of the person it is necessary for the robot to keep the person in sight. This component searches for an OOL near the person by using the previously calculated safety factors. This also assures the person staying in sight so that the observation can continue.

Searching for the Person. The target of the observation is the person. If the person it out of sight, the robot waits a few minutes (configurable for personal

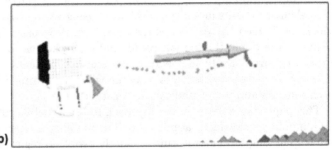

Fig. 5. a) Picture of the used robot; b) Person walking in front of the robot with calculated direction indicated by an arrow

convenience) for the person to come back before moving away from its current position. The first step is to search and find the person by guessing where it could be. The first position which is searched is the last known and therefore the last detected position. Starting at that location the robot moves into the last known direction of the person. It is assumed that the robot is being used in a domestic home with limited size. With the help of the map the robot knows which area is left to search. If the person is still not found at the end of a search phase the robot returns to its base position.

Observation Position. Once the person is found all fields within a certain range are checked for a good safety value (OOL). All fields above a certain value are potential fields. So all potential fields are checked and compared by the number of visible fields. The robot is placed on the field with the highest value.

Pseudo code of user observation algorithm

```
method UserObservation (User_positions pos)
    if (userRecognized = true)
      reset timer;
    else
      timer++;

    if (timer > recognitionThreshold)
      move_Robot(pos.last_known_user_position);
      if (userRecognized = true)
        move_Robot(next_OOL_position); reset timer;
      else
        move_Robot(pos.last_known_direction_of_user)
end method
```

6 Discussion

Mobility is one of the most important factors influencing an independent lifestyle and perceived quality of life. Especially elderly people suffer from reduced mobility and require care mostly due to mobility problems. Therefore, estimation of remaining mobility is an essential part of each geriatric assessment. Within clinical environments mobility is evaluated using various assessment tests among which the 'Timed Up and Go' is the most frequently used. Bringing such assessments to the domestic domain could enable physicians to provide earlier diagnosis, to prevent acute incidents or to monitor patients during rehabilitation at home. However, assessments at home will be performed in non-standardized environments and under unclear circumstances.

This paper presented a novel approach to use a mobile robot platform as base for a mobility assessment application. The mobility assessment on the one hand can help in long term monitoring of elderly people in regard to recognize diseases and increased fall risks. On the other hand, the assessed movement data and profiles of the observed person can also be used to enhance the robot's navigation and observation capabilities. The medical background and technical development has been described. To the best of our current knowledge, this approach is unique. Initial results show that the algorithms produce reasonable data. At the time of writing, further more intensive tests are ongoing and planned. The next step will be to move the robot in a real user environment, i.e. bringing the robot into an elderly person's home.

Acknowledgments. This work was partially funded under the 7th EC Framework Programme within the Florence project (ICT-2009-248730).

References

1. Committee on Quality of Health Care in America, Institute of Medicine: Crossing the Quality Chasm: A New Health System for the 21st Century, 1st edn. National Academies Press (2001)
2. European Commission Research: Seventh Framework - Work Programme 2011-2012, ICT (2010)
3. Frenken, T., Növercin, M., Mersmann, S., Hein, A.: Precise Assessment of Self-Selected Gait Velocity in Domestic Environments. In: Pervasive Computing Technologies for Healthcare, PervasiveHealth (2010)
4. Butler, A.A., Menant, J.C., Tiedemann, A.C., Lord, S.R.: Age and gender differences in seven tests of functional mobility. Journal of NeuroEngineering and Rehabilitation 6, 31 (2009)
5. Alzheimer's Disease International: Alzheimer's Disease International: World Alzheimer Report 2009. Online (2009)
6. Beauchet, O., Allali, G., Berrut, G., Hommet, C., Dubost, V., Assal, F.: Gait analysis in demented subjects: Interests and perspectives. Neuropsychiatric Disease and Treatment 4(1), 155–160 (2008)
7. Scanaill, C.N., Carew, S., Barralon, P., Noury, N., Lyons, D., Lyons, G.M.: A review of approaches to mobility telemonitoring of the elderly in their living environment. Annals of Biomedical Engineering 34(4), 547–563 (2006)
8. Cameron, K., Hughes, K., Doughty, K.: Reducing fall incidence in community elders by telecare using predictive systems. In: Proc. 19th Annual International Conference of the IEEE Engineering in Medicine and Biology Society, vol. 3, pp. 1036–1039 (1997)

9. Kaye, J.A., Maxwell, S.A., Mattek, N., Hayes, T.L., Dodge, H., Pavel, M., Jimison, H.B., Wild, K., Boise, L., Zitzelberger, T.A.: Intelligent Systems for Assessing Aging Changes: home-based, unobtrusive, and continuous assessment of aging. The Journals of Gerontology. Series B, Psychological Sciences and Social Sciences 66(supp. 1), i180–i190 (2011)

10. Pallejà, T., Teixidó, M., Tresanchez, M., Palacín, J.: Measuring Gait Using a Ground Laser Range Sensor. Sensors 9(11), 9133–9146 (2009)

11. Zhou, H., Hu, H.: Human motion tracking for rehabilitation: A survey. Biomedical Signal Processing and Control 3(1), 1–18 (2008)

12. Bachmann, C., Gerber, H., Stacoff, A.: Messsysteme, Messmethoden und Beispiele zur instrumentierten Ganganalyse. Schweizerische Zeitschrift für Sportmedizin und Sporttraumatologie 56(2), 29–34 (2008)

13. Zijlstra, W., Hof, A.L.: Assessment of spatio-temporal gait parameters from trunk accelerations during human walking. Gait & Posture 18(2), 1–10 (2003)

14. Aminian, K., Najafi, B., Böla, C., Leyvraz, P.F., Robert, P.: Spatio-temporal parameters of gait measured by an ambulatory system using miniature gyroscopes. Journal of Biomechanics 35(5), 689–699 (2002)

15. Liu, J., Lockhart, T.E., Jones, M., Martin, T.: Local Dynamic Stability Assessment of Motion Impaired Elderly Using Electronic Textile Pants. IEEE Transactions on Automation Science and Engineering 5(4), 696–702 (2008)

16. Frenken, T., Brell, M., Gövercin, M., Wegel, S., Hein, A.: aTUG: technical apparatus for gait and balance analysis within component-based Timed Up & Go using mutual ambient sensors. Journal of Ambient Intelligence and Humanized Computing (July 2012)

17. Van der Loos, H.F.M., Hammel, J., Leifer, L.J.: DeVAR transfer from R&D to vocational and educational settings. In: Proc. Fourth International Conference on Rehabilitation Robotics, pp. 151–156 (1994)

18. Matsumoto, Y., Ino, T., Ogasawara, T.: Development of intelligent wheelchair system with face and gaze based interface. In: Proceedings of 10th IEEE Int. Workshop on Robot and Human Communication (ROMAN 2001), pp. 262–267 (2001)

19. Reiser, U., Connette, C., Fischer, J., Kubacki, J., Bubeck, A., Weisshardt, F., Jacobs, T., Parlitz, C., Högele, M., Verl, A.: Care-O-bot 3 - Creating a product vision for service robot applications by integrating design and technology. In: The 2009 IEEE/RSJ International Conference on Intelligent Robots and Systems, pp. 1992–1997 (2009)

20. Cesta, A., Cortellessa, G., Giuliani, M.V., Pecora, F., Scopelliti, M., Tiberio, L.: Psychological implications of domestic assistive technology for the elderly. Psych-Nology Journal 5, 229–252 (2007)

21. Quigley, M., Gerkey, B., Conley, K., Faust, J., Foote, T., Leibs, J., Berger, E., Wheeler, R., Ng, A.: ROS: an open-source Robot Operating System. In: ICRA Workshop on Open Source Software, vol. 3 (2009)

22. Frenken, T., Isken, M., Volkening, N., Brell, M., Hein, A.: Criteria for Quality and Safety while Performing Unobtrusive Domestic Mobility Assessments using Mobile Service Robots. In: Wichert, R., Eberhardt, B. (eds.) Ambient Assisted Living. Advanced Technologies and Societal Change, pp. 61–76. Springer, Heidelberg (2012)

A GPS/Wi-Fi/Marker Analysis Based Simultaneous and Hierarchical Multi-Positioning System

Akram Salem, Philippe Canalda, and François Spies

Institut FEMTO-ST UMR CNRS 6174, Département d'Informatique des Systèmes Complexes / Optimization Mobility NetworkIng Team, 1, Cours Louis Leprince-Ringuet 25200 Montbéliard - France
{Philippe.Canalda,Akram.Salem,Francois.Spies}@femto-st.fr

Abstract. The SHMPS system, to be presented and experimented at EvAAL 2013, is composed of, first of all a hierarchical positioning algorithm which manage a multi-positioning system composed of a GPS positioning system, a Wi-Fi based fingerprinting and trilateration system, and a marker analysis system. As soon as the latter system can provide localization information, the precedent running system switches to a learning process. The hypothesis, when running the multi-positioning system in successive outdoor and indoor environments is that the marker analysis based positioning is more accurate than Wi-Fi trilateration based one, which is more accurate than GPS' one. Our SHMPS (Simultaneous & Hierarchical Multi-Positioning System) system proposal, to compete this year to EvAAL 2013 benchmarking competition, is a stand-alone application embedded on a smart mobile device equipped with camera. This initial version associates the standard GPS application with either WIFISLAM or our OwlPS system and a natural and artificial marker analysis based on FATE or NyArtoolkit libraries. The gaps of accuracy then performed allow to switch from 8 meters outside to 4 to 5 meters inside and finally to decimeters when the instantaneous marker analysis is performing well. The hierarchical organization provides a practical way to handle the contextual download of marker information needed.

Keywords: marker analysis, multi-positioning system, hybrid positioning algorithm, GPS, Wi-Fi network, fingerprinting method, RSSI cartography.

1 A Multi-Configuration Wi-Fi Based Multi-Positioning System to Improve Localization Continuity and to Perform Multi-scale Localization

The OMNI[1] team has been engaged in a positioning program initiated by the Pays de Montbéliard Agglomération, since 2006.

---

[1] OMNI stands for Optimization Mobility and NetworkIng. OMNI is a team from the DISC Department of Femto-st Institute.

J.A. Botía et al. (Eds.): EvAAL 2013, CCIS 386, pp. 106–116, 2013.
© Springer-Verlag Berlin Heidelberg 2013

The focus is on Wi-Fi based positioning techniques and algorithms applied to hostile environment. Two kinds of architectures have been studied, first, in a former phase, a Mobile Terminal (MT) centric one, and in a later phase, an infrastructure centric one. Several techniques and algorithms from the literature have been developed and integrated into an internal development suite, so that simulations, emulations and real experimentations are conducted following scenarios inside modern building and across indoor and canyon urban environments.

1.1 History and Internal Related Works: Outdoor/Indoor Continuous Localization, Wi-Fi Access Points Optimization Placement, Automatic Calibration ...

When, at the very beginning the system architecture was terminal centric, indoor positioning researches dealt with Wi-Fi positioning or GPS-based positioning. Since 2008, the architecture has become infrastructure-centric oriented, reducing the application part to being embedded in any MT, focusing on intrusive or non-intrusive localization, or on the illicit use of wireless network. Hence research activities have addressed combined positioning such as GPS and Wi-Fi in indoor environment, to improve the positioning service coverage significantly. Since 2010, we have investigated how to switch from one positioning system to another and how to dimension heterogeneous Wi-Fi infrastructure by adapting geometric and attenuation signal strength dilution of precision criteria.

Two years ago, we have competed with the 2nd evolution of our Wi-Fi based Positioning System named "OwlPS". Among the most innovative functionalities of this 1.2 version of OwlPS, the auto-calibration functionality reduces the off-line RSSI fingerprinting phase to the minimum.

Last year, we have also competed. The system proposed was, first of all enriched with dynamic change exploitation that means not only the last up-to-date RSSI- fingerprinting calibration, but also the instantaneous RSSI variation due mainly to human presence. Therein, the loss of the line of sight between Wi-Fi Access Points (AP for short) and MT or the abnormal attenuation of signal strength between various reference points dynamically configured the K-angle-weighted neighbourhood algorithm proposed. Second, the RSSI cartography modelled the orientation of MT and the relative positioning of human. Third a tuning of OwlPS system development kit was performed in an off-line phase. It made use of a 3D dimensioning tool placing N-APs according to a GDOP_RSSI n-loss criteria and COST-231 propagation model. It also made use of a smartphone Android-based functionality to calibrate on-demand AOI reference points.

1.2 New Problems Addressed Bridging the Gap from Decametric Precision to Sub Metric Precision

This year, the system has been enriched with, first of all a hierarchical positioning algorithm which manage a multi-positioning system composed of a GPS positioning system, a Wi-Fi based fingerprinting and tri-lateration system, and a marker analysis system. As soon as the latter system can provide localization information, the precedent running system switches to a learning process.

1.3   Summary of Our Proposal

In the sequel, we will briefly describe the core OwlPS system which has competed to EvAAL'11. We will summarize also the techniques and algorithms which have been conceived, developed and experimented in real experiments during the last decade, such as the [16] navigator monitoring interface. Then we will also describe briefly the contributions to EvAAL'12 which may use of dynamic changes from radio-environment, the K-Weighted-Neighbourhood algorithm, the smart Android Interface to better pilot calibrations processes and adaptive real-time positioning, and the 3D dimensioning tooling.

After that we will present our SHMPS, our new contributions. SHMPS stands for Simultaneous & Hierarchical Multi-Positioning System.

Finally we will discuss internal laboratory experiments and dress the perspectives of our proposal on a scientific view and on the EvAAL'13 competition view.

2   OwlPS 1.2 Version which Competed at EvAAL'11: A Wi-Fi Based Infrastructure Centric Positioning System

2.1   OwlPS Core Architecture

The OwlPS is an indoor positioning system based on the IEEE 802.11 radio network (Wi-Fi). It mainly exploits RSSI fingerprinting and indoor propagation models, helped by information such as the map of the building, the mobile path, etc. Fingerprinting location approaches provide a 4 meter mean error for a 3-D positioning, with only 5 Wi-Fi access points deployed in an area of 300m². The previous version of the system includes a self-calibration mechanism, which avoids the time-consuming manual fingerprinting phase.

The architecture of Owl Positioning System is infrastructure-centered. We first present its architecture and its deployment process, then the positioning algorithms implemented, and finally an explanation of the self-calibration mechanism. As summarized in Fig. 1, OwlPS is composed of several elements:

- Mobile terminals, such as laptops, PDAs, cell phones, hand-held game consoles, etc., which are equipped with Wi-Fi cards. These run the owlps-client software, which is a classical UDP/IP application.
- Access points (APs), which capture the frames of the Wi-Fi network by listening for any positioning request transmitted by the mobiles. These run the owlps-listener software, which uses the pcap library to capture the IEEE 802.11 frames. The SS values are extracted from the Radiotap [4] header of each frame; therefore the network interface driver must support Radiotap [5]. It is possible to have as many APs as desired: as long as they are only listening to the radio network, they do not cause any interference.
- The aggregation server, to which the APs forward the captured positioning requests; its task is to gather and format these requests. It runs the owlps-aggregator software.
- The positioning server (or computation server), which computes the position of each mobile from the information forwarded by the aggregation server, thanks to the owlps-positioner software.

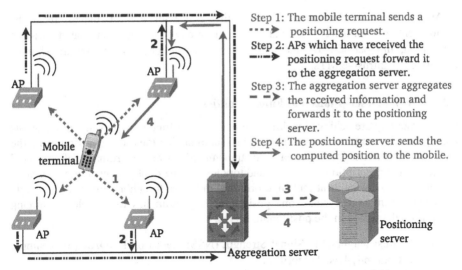

Step 1: The mobile terminal sends a positioning request.

Step 2: APs which have received the positioning request forward it to the aggregation server.

Step 3: The aggregation server aggregates the received information and forwards it to the positioning server.

Step 4: The positioning server sends the computed position to the mobile.

Fig. 1. OwlPS infrastructure-centric architecture and Signal Strength acquisition process

2.2 The OwlPS Processes: Dynamic Signal Strength Cartography, Cyclic Localization

The Signal Strength Acquisition process (SSA-process for short) is used during the (auto-) calibration phase and the positioning/tracking phase. It helps to build the Signal Strength Cartography (SSC for short) from the signal transmitted either by an AP to other Aps or an MT to all APs. The auto-calibration phase eliminates the costly off-line calibration of fingerprinting based positioning algorithm. In this previous version of OwlPS, the auto-calibration is executed recurrently, according to a time period. A token ring-based algorithm assigns to each AP the right to deliver an explicit calibration packet to the aggregator. The positioning functionality runs under two modes, an explicit one and an implicit one. The former requires the MT to send a packet in a specific format [13], whereas the latter accepts any UDP-like packets which are intercepted and analyzed by APs, then transmitted to the aggregator. Hence the aggregator temporally collapses the SS received and transmits it to the calculator which computes the SS tuple respectful of an off-line configuration. The tuple represents the t means of n UDP packets transmitted by either an AP or the MT, with t the number of Aps (each visible by (t-1) others). m tuples are registered in an SSC, with m the size of the grid depending on the distance between each RP in a 2D-plan. As an illustration, if we consider[2] a rectangular room of l by L m^2, where $l = 5.8$ m., and $L = 10.6$ m., then the number of RPs nbRP= $(l+1)*(L+1)$, considering a grid meshing of 1 m.

---

[2] This room is located in our Multimedia Development Center NUMERICA, at the -1 level, our laboratory used this space to experiment automatic indoor AR-Drone navigation, and also to evaluate the optimal sizing and positioning of APs, and also to design and compare the techniques and algorithm of positioning.

Around the SSA-Process, numerous other processes are articulated, from the deployment of infrastructure and its configuration to the automated off-line calibration, the periodic on-line auto-calibration, the positioning and tracking of authorized or intrusive MTs.

2.3   OwlPS Descriptions and Functionalities

These processes are achieved making use of a bulk of functionalities and descriptions among which: wired and wireless 802.11.x communications, the description of the hardware characteristics (antenna gain, transmitted power, coordinates of the fixed elements), the description of the size and topology of the deployment area if available, and manual on-line calibration (fingerprinting) only if auto-calibration is not selected,

When running the system, one positioning algorithm has to be selected among several[3] implemented in the positioning server:

- Nearest neighbor in Signal Strength (NSS), based on RADAR [3], a simple cartography-based algorithm.
- Trilateration using the propagation formula proposed by Interlink Networks [1].
- Trilateration using the FBCM [2, 7] (Friis-Based Calibrated Model), which adapts the propagation formula to match the deployment area's characteristics better.
- Basic FRBHM [8, 7, 9] (FBCM and Reference-Based Hybrid Model), a combination of the NSS and the FBCM which allows to adapt the propagation formula dynamically to the characteristics of the room where the MT is supposed to be.

2.4   OwlPS Techniques and Tool Set Box

When designing and developing a new positioning algorithm, some other techniques are usable to serve as a basis or to compare performance such as support for the Viterbi-enabled algorithms:

- NSS with Viterbi-like [10],
- Discrete and Continuous FRBHM [7, 9].

At the very first competition EvAAL'11, we presented a Wi-Fi based navigation monitoring and, in addition, an AR-Drone navigator using an itinerary scenario description [13].

3   At EvAAL'12, OwlPS Version Exploits the Dynamic Changes of the Radio Environment Better

OwlPS implements an auto-calibration mechanism that allows the system to be operational within a few seconds after its deployment. Since the self-calibration is a

---

[3] These algorithms were described and compared in [6].

continuous process, it also guarantees that the system is aware of the modifications occurring in the radio environment. In the previous competition, we proved that the self-calibration process annihilates the costly previous off-line calibration phase, without altering the accuracy of the positioning (for a mean accuracy of 4m, for 4 APs deployed in the competition area). The positioning server builds a matrix of the SSs received by each APRx from each APTx (with Rx and Tx $\in$ [1,N] and N the number of deployed APs). Several matrixes are computed:

Table 1. OwlPS' result at EvAAL'2012 Competition

Positioning System evaluated	Accuracy	Availability	Installation complexity	User's acceptance	Integrability in AAL	Final Score and rank
OwlPS 1.3 Version	0,8	10	9,7	6,4	6,9	6,29 3rd/7

- MAPs represent the SSC of APs. We recommend to register an initial one, iMAP, performed when no human is present in the experimentation area, and another incrementally modified one of MAPs (CurrentTime) for which the refreshing period can be parameterized to 4 per second. Then, the Radio-Environment Sensible Positioning Algorithm (RESP-algorithm for short) being invoked at CurrentTime consecutively to an explicit positioning demand from an MT, the RESP-algorithm first identifies which APRx-APTx is attenuated when differentiating iMAPs with MAPs(CurrentTime), and second the relative positioning of the MT with the human presence. Then the K-angle weighted neighborhood (KAWN) algorithm [13] is more appropriately applied.
- MAPs+RPs represent the SSC of APs and RPs. The SSC of RPs is obtained by applying the KAWN algorithm considering a position of a virtual MT M which matches the RPs position defined from the topology of the experimentation area and the meshing of the SSC's grid.

The KAWN algorithm is extended when identifying a rupture of the line of sight between two APs, and considering where the human could be positioned when using the MT being tracked.

A Smart Android Interface suited to Wi-Fi indoor positioning data repository (OwlPs-SAI for short) has been designed and developed. From OwlPS version 1.2, experimenting any new OwlPS version based system of indoor positioning, the deployment is guided when configuring the refreshing frequency of any SSCs, calibration is performed on demand, either automatically or manually. The manual calibration allows inserting a specific RP or modifying one, and it may be previously set during the initial auto-calibration phase. The MT interface proposes two modes of interaction, a declarative one, and a smart-sensor one. The Wi-Fi indoor positioning data repository is extended (see Fig.4) with the orientation and positioning of both the APs, and the MTs. The relative positioning of the human is registered depending on either the explicit declaration or the sensor equipment available on the MT. Last but not least, data repository synchronization is performed between the SQLite local data repository on the MT, and the distant SQL-based server-side data repository. This is more robust in the face of any Wi-Fi communication disturbances, and respectful of the privacy and confidentiality of the user's data.

The OwlPS system is completed by other tools. The last decade positioning program has provided our team with a geometric and SS attenuation dilution of precision criteria for the Wi-Fi positioning system combined or not with a GPS positioning system. With this in mind, we have modeled and implemented a 2D AP placement optimizer. It optimizes the geometric positioning of APs and its impact on the indoor positioning accuracy. A study has been performed in a real room inside our laboratory, sustained by a simulation platform which involves:

- Radio propagation models such as Friis and COST231-Hata.
- The planning of the Wi-Fi network inside an indoor 2D topology, with or without walls. We will exploit this tool to determine how many APs can be used and where to position them in order to optimize both the maximal and mean Wi-Fi GDOP values.

4   At EvAAL'13, OwlPS Version 1.3 Based Simultaneous and Hierarchical Multi-Positioning System Competes

This year, the system has been enriched with, first of all a hierarchical positioning algorithm which manages a multi-positioning system composed of a GPS positioning system, a Wi-Fi based fingerprinting and tri-lateration system, and a marker analysis system.

As soon as the latter system can provide localisation information, the precedent running system switches to a learning process.

The hypothesis, when running the multi-positioning system in successive outdoor and indoor environments is that the marker analysis based positioning is more accurate than Wi-Fi tri-lateration based one, which is more accurate than GPS' one. Our SHMPS (Simultaneous & Hierarchical Multi-Positioning System) system proposal, to compete this year to EvAAL 2013 benchmarking competition, is a stand-alone application embedded on a smart mobile device equipped with camera (see figure Fig 2).

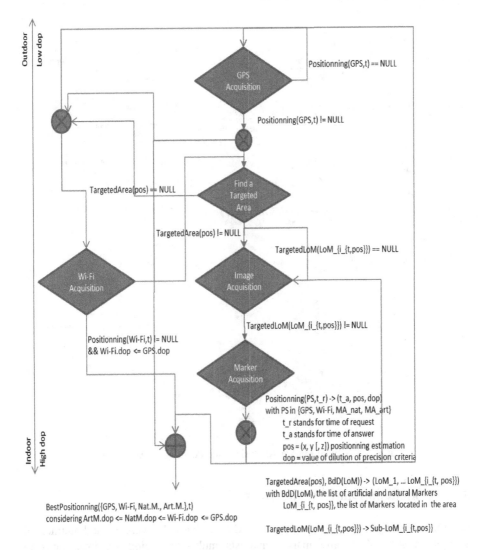

Fig. 2. Hierarchical Multi-Positioning Algorithm

This initial version associate the standard GPS application with either WIFISLAM or our OwlPS system and a natural and artificial marker analysis based on FATE or NyArtoolkit libraries. Figure 2 shows the logical diagram of the Hierarchical Multi-Positioning Algorithm implemented. Figure 3 details the Artificial Marker Analysis based positioning Algorithm.

The gaps of accuracy then performed allow to switch from 8 meters outside to 4 to 5 meters inside and finally to decimetres [15] when the instantaneous marker analysis is performing well.

The hierarchical organization provides a practical way to handle the contextual download of marker information needed.

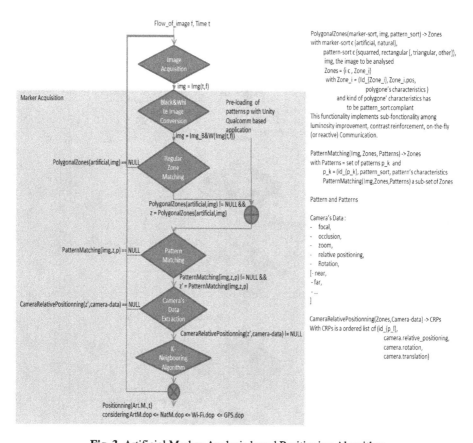

Fig. 3. Artificial Marker Analysis based Positioning Algorithm

5   Conclusion and Perspectives

Our Our current proposal composed of the OwlPS' latest 1.3 version, and augmented with hierarchical GPS and marker analysis multi-positioning systems, tends to improve OwlPS v1.3 which has competed last year and obtain the 3rd position.

This new version proposed is more robust to wide area and also provide a good accuracy where luminosity is suitable.

A very first version of this system has been experimented outdoor, since May 2012, to provide a multimedia guide to assist during Mandeure Roman Amphitheatre reality augmented visit.

Acknowledgement. The authors want to thank Matteo Cypriani, Soumaya Zirari, Hakim Mabed, Honoré Bizagwira, Nicolas Boillot, Mouhannad Kazmouz, Florian Bataillard which contribute to produce the multi-positioning prototype, and the optimizing and placing libraries. This work has been, for part, supported by the Pays de Montbéliard Agglomeration and the European project G-Navis FP7 Collaborative Project, grant agreement No. 287203.

References

1. Interlink Networks, Inc.: A practical approach to identifying and tracking unauthorized 802.11 cards and access points. TR (2002)
2. Lassabe, F., Baala, O., Canalda, P., Chatonnay, P., Spies, F.: A Friis-based calibrated model for WiFi terminals positioning. In: Proceedings of IEEE Int. Symp. on a World of Wireless, Mobile and Multimedia Networks, Taormina, Italy, pp. 382–387 (June 2005)
3. Bahl, P., Padmanabhan, V.N.: RADAR: An in-building RF-based user location and tracking system. In: INFOCOM (2), pp. 775–784 (2000)
4. Radiotap website: http://www.radiotap.org/ (last access to the web content June 12, 2013)
5. Radiotap on Linux Wireless website: http://linuxwireless.org/en/developers/Documentation/radiotap (last access to the web content June 12, 2013)
6. Cypriani, M., Lassabe, F., Canalda, P., Spies, F.: Open Wireless Positioning System: a Wi-Fi-based indoor positioning system. In: VTC-fall 2009, 70th IEEE Vehicular Technology Conference, Anchorage, Alaska, IEEE Vehicular Technology Society (September 2009)

7. Lassabe, F., Canalda, P., Chatonnay, P., Spies, F.: Indoor Wi-Fi positioning: Techniques and systems. Annals of Telecommunications 64(9/10), 651–664 (2009)

8. Lassabe, F., Charlet, D., Canalda, P., Chatonnay, P., Spies, F.: Refining WiFi indoor positioning renders pertinent deploying location-based multimedia guide. In: Proceedings of IEEE 20th Int. Conf. on Advanced Information Networking and Applications, Vienna, Austria, vol. 2, pp. 126–130 (April 2006)

9. Cypriani, M., Canalda, P., Lassabe, F., Spies, F.: Wi-Fi-based indoor positioning: Basic techniques, hybrid algorithms and open software platform. In: Mautz, R., Kunz, M., Ingensand, H. (eds.) IPIN 2010, IEEE Int. Conf. on Indoor Positioning and Indoor Navigation, Switzerland, pp. 116–125 (September 2010)

10. Bahl, P., Balachandran, A., Padmanabhan, V.: Enhancements to the RADAR user location and tracking system. Technical report, Microsoft Research (February 2000)

11. MadWifi website: http://www.madwifi-project.org/

12. Cypriani, M., Canalda, P., Zirari, S., Lassabe, F., Spies, F.: Open Wireless Positioning System, version 0.8. Technical Report RT2008-02, LIFC – Laboratoire d'Informatique de l'Université de Franche Comté (December 2008)

13. Cypriani, M., Canalda, P., Spies, F.: OwlPS: A Self-calibrated Fingerprint-Based Wi-Fi Positioning. In: Chessa, S., Knauth, S. (eds.) EvAAL 2011. CCIS, vol. 309, pp. 36–51. Springer, Heidelberg (2012); Note: Revised selected paper from the International Competition EvAAL 2011, Competition in Valencia, Spain, July 2011, and Final Workshop in Lecce, Italy, September 2011

14. Cypriani, M., Canalda, P., Spies, F., Ancuta, D.: Benchmark Measurements for Wi-Fi Signal Strength based Positioning System. In: Rizos, C., Mautz, R. (eds.) IPIN 2012, Int. Conf. on Indoor Positioning and Indoor Navigation, Sydney, Australia, 8 pages. IEEE (November 2012)

15. Canalda, P., Salem, A., Spies, F., Tabbane, S.: An IMA-based Centimeter Precise Positioning for Smart Mobile Devices in Hostile Environments. In: Rizos, C., Mautz, R. (eds.) IPIN 2012, Int. Conf. on Indoor Positioning and Indoor Navigation, Sydney, Australia, 5 pages. IEEE (November 2012)

16. Parrot Ar-Drone specification: http://ardrone.parrot.com/parrot-ar-drone/en/technologies (last access to the web content June 12, 2013)

Indoor Localization and Tracking Using 802.11 Networks and Smartphones

João Quintas[1,*], António Cunha[1], Pedro Serra[1], André Pereira[1], Bruno Marques[1], and Jorge Dias[2,3]

[1] Laboratory of Automatics and Systems of Instituto Pedro Nunes, Portugal
{jquintas,cunha,pfserra,apereira,bmarques}@ipn.pt
[2] Universidade de Coimbra, Portugal
jorge@deec.uc.pt
[3] Khalifa University, Abu Dhabi

Abstract. ambient assisted living is an area of interest because of the potential for aid in needs and difficulties for the elderly or disabled. These systems have the potential to help control medication intake up to saving lives by complex monitoring. In this type of monitoring, an indoor localization system is necessary. We propose an indoor localization system based on existing WiFi networks, which doubles as a platform to store positional data. This is implemented through location fingerprinting with added value and precision.

Keywords: indoor, location, position, wifi, gps, signal strength, navigation, calibration, user, phone, mobile, device, positioning, localization.

1 Introduction

The human longevity is increasing and we are facing a reality of an elderly population that needs special care. The ambient assisted living aims to step up to this challenge, assisting people with needs and assist them in different situations.

Within a living spaceequipped with different kind of sensors, the user's actions and behaviors can provide useful information about their needs and indicate an eventual emergency situation.As a lot of these needsare directly related to the location of the user, knowing its location in a system is the problem that this technology is covering, helping elderly people with positioning awareness problems and enabling some caregivers to overview the activities and problems of those users, taking the appropriate actions to help them [1].Knowingthe users position, the caregivers can mergethis information with other information from sensors and filter false positives alarms etc.

2 State of theArt

Several different approaches for indoor localization exist, using a variety of technologies such as ultrasonic sound, UWB radio, RFID, Bluetooth, Infrared, Wi-Fi, etc. These approaches mostly require extrahardware or software on the devices and

J.A. Botía et al. (Eds.): EvAAL 2013, CCIS 386, pp. 117–127, 2013.

installation site, increasing the cost and complexity of deployment significantly. Solutions that use existing hardware capabilities, like Bluetooth and Wi-Fi, severely reduce concerns about complexity and cost, especially in the case of Wi-Fi where an existing network can be used as beacon sources for localization.

Commercial solutions using a similar approach already exist. For example the CISCO localization framework which provides great accuracy but is based on expensive proprietary hardware, which is required to be the sole wireless network provider as well as internal cabled networks. Other commercial solutions, such as Ekahau can indeed use an existing network and work on a cloud based system to deliver real-time localization.

3   Proposed Solution

For the development of this solution, an indoor positioning system that uses Wi-Fi information that is available at cheap prices has beenchosen, in that it already exists in almost every household. Even if the target network needs improvements, it can be made with very affordable prices and the system is able to track most mobile devices that have Wi-Fi connection and can run simple application.

In the presented solution we have developed an application for mobile phones that uses Android OS, localization techniques and server side logic to do the localization inside buildings.A general overview of the system's architecture can be seen in Fig.1.

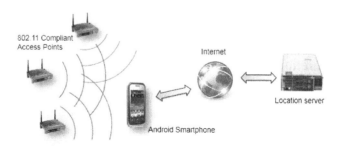

Fig. 1. System architecture overview

The hardware needed for the presented solution is described below:

- A mobile device, capable of running simple applications with access to the wireless signals. The present solution currently requires an Android device with version 2.1 of the OS or better, with a very light application that can run easily on the majority of existing Android smartphones.
- A wireless network with several 802.11 compatible access points. Additional access points may be required for a stable localization system, but existing access points can all be reused.
- Network access to the localization server in the mobile device, either through the existing Wi-Fi network or using a mobile data service.

4   Used Protocols

The technology relies mostly on the 802.11 Wi-Fi standard networks, routers, access points and client devices. The only exploited part of the protocol is the use of the access points broadcast beacon, reading its BSSID (Basic Service Set Identification) and RSSI (Received Signal Strength Indicator).

To communicate with the location server, a SOAP (Simple Object Access Protocol) interface is used to expose web services that provide the required methods for calibration and localization routines.An example illustrating the location process and communications flow can be seen in Fig.2.

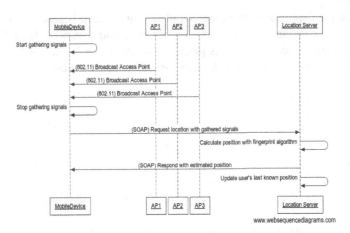

Fig. 2. Sequence diagram illustrating the location process

5   Deployment

The deployment of the systems needs basically two 2 steps, installation and calibration.

5.1   Installation

For the installation the wireless emitters (access points) are either installed after assessment, have to be rearranged or simply the existing network setup can be reused. Network connectivity within the network is not a requirement, but is an option, as a mobile phone can make use of all "visible" routers and use its mobile data connection instead of connecting to the local network.

5.2   Calibration

During the calibration, information of the respective rooms, etc., has to be mapped with the network signals, information which will later be used for the localization process.

This calibration typically consists of one or multiple human installers roaming the location with a calibration application (on a mobile phone), marking their current location on a map and activating a reading and calibration procedure with one touch. When all of the intended calibration spots are done, the system can do the data processing required to enhance to localization reach and precision.

The process of calibration is simple, the user with the device will have to go to the specific points of the floor plan, and select the space value where he is and then he just has to select the option to calibrate. During this calibration, a lot of data is recorded: all the readings from the different access points, an average of all the readings for each access point, the standard deviation for the readings and the number of samples for each reading.

When all the deployment steps are completed, the system is ready to be used and track the users' positions. This information can be remotely viewed through a testing web page created especially for this purpose (shown in Fig.3). In this web page, all the latest known user locations can be seen placed on the floor map.

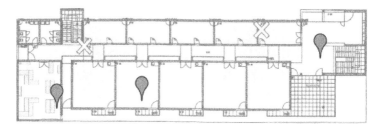

Fig. 3. Test web site showing multiple users' locations

6   Algorithms

There are twokey algorithms used in the system: spatial data interpolation within the calibrated buildings and localization fingerprinting.

The spatial data interpolation makes use of sparse linear algebra and partial differential equation discretization to enhance and fill the spatial data, providing fingerprinting through localization information overa whole building's floor plans without the need to physically calibrate every possible position.

The basis for the system to work is the location fingerprinting, which compares the calibrated points to the real time readings of the device to be located (see equation 1) [2] [4]. This comparison and selection uses the RSSI values and processes them based on the location and thestandard deviation of the same signal and value, includingthe selection process making use of a weighted kNN (k Nearest Neighbor) solution. We select the best k positions and give them different weights based on the metric. With that information we can calculate a weighted mean of the k positions. Another good part of this method is that it cleans a few inaccurate position estimationsgiven by the algorithm.

$$D(x,y) = \sum_{k=0}^{n} |meanRSSI(k)_x - RSSI_y| \tag{1}$$

If the system will use a non-processed calibration, without the spatial data interpolation, it means that it will only have the real calibrations done by the device. With the real calibration we have information about standard deviation from the signals of the access points.

In this case we use a Euclidean Distance based on the information of the standard deviation made in the calibration. We apply the weight of the standard deviation in the formula to balance the variations of the signals in fingerprinting [4].

$$D(x,y) = \sum_{k=x}^{n} \frac{1}{w_{xy}} |meanRSSI(k)_x - RSSI_y| \tag{2}$$

A second option is made with an inverse weight, where we utilize all the available information that can improve a precision increase in the results given by the following formula [4].

$$D(x,y) = \frac{1}{\sum_{x=0}^{n} w_x} \sum_{k=x}^{n} w_y |meanRSSI(k)_x - RSSI_y| \tag{3}$$

After the results of the localization algorithm, a Kalman state is used to smooth the movement of the object in two dimensions and append inertia for short-term predictive positioning, all using the localization updates as they are generated in the device-system.

7   Internal Data

The internal data producedandstored in a remote database for exclusive use includes:

- Recorded routers/access points, which are used in the calibration/localization process.
- Map information, such as buildings, floor plans and their geological placement, i.e. global coordinates.
- Calibration points, which store location and visible routers, including BSSID, RSSI and its standard deviation.
- User location information, updated with each successful localization.

An example of the stored internal data is shown in Table 1, illustrating the recorded access points for several coordinates.

Table 1. Example of stored access point readings for several locations

Location Id	AP 1 (dBm)	AP 2 (dBm)	AP 3 (dBm)	AP 4 (dBm)
1	-49,2	-51,2	-52,4	-72,2
2	-65,0	-81,2	-71,6	-82,4
3	-37,0	-38,4	-76,2	-85,8
4	-47,0	-86,0	-49,0	-61,6
5	-49,4	-69,4	-65,6	-69,6

Data Description

The internal data includes the calibration points' data. This is the source data that will be processed, using the previously described algorithms, which results in data of the same type as the calibration data, replacing all the source data and filling in to a broader location reach with higher precision.

With the calibration points, as seen in an example floor in Fig. 4, several signal strength maps can be constructed, one for each access point.

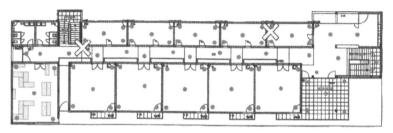

Fig. 4. Example of a calibration map, the red dots mark the calibrated spots

Each map is then processed using previously described algorithm, which includes interpolation an extrapolation from all the available data to the full extent of the floor map. The resulting processed signal strength map for one access point from the calibration spots in Fig. 4 can be seen in Fig. 5. This map was chosen as an example because the access point is "visible" through the whole floor and thus represents a fairly complete signal strength map.

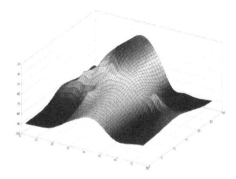

Fig. 5. Example signal strength map, x and y are the positions, the z is the signal strength

After the entire floor plan is created, we need to clean some extrapolated information that is actually harmful to the localization algorithm. Besides occupyingunnecessary processor time, it is unnecessary and an inaccurate estimation. This is a side-effect of the processing algorithm and must be dealt with.

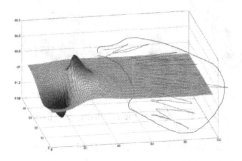

Fig. 6. Signal strength map with bad data crossed out in red. X and Y are the positions, Z is the signal strength.

In our approach this is done by filtering the data validity by a radius of real calibration points. A trust distance was used to know when to cut-off the estimated data. To define this trusted distance, several tests and empirical observation (Fig. 7) from a small data set of calibrations, from the left to the right we have the radius in the filter going larger every time.

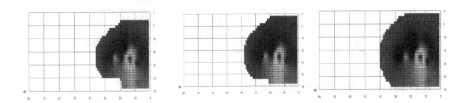

Fig. 7. Trusted radius of estimated readings, with increasing radius from left to right. X and y are the position coordinates in the floor plan.

This kind of technique is very important for the offline version of the application to save battery and improve the time that the calculation needs to give a final position.

In the Fig. 8we can see two examples of the resulting maps strengths for two floor plans, one where all data passed the trusted radius and on where some of the extrapolations where cut due to being outside the trusted radius of non-estimated readings.

The internal data produced for each user, consist of the position and the time that the certain position has been calculated. There are two types of tables that save the user information. The simple one only has the ID of the building and the last position

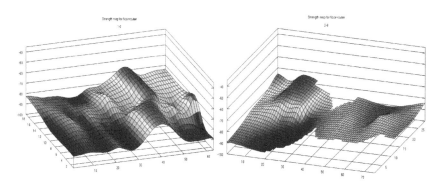

Fig. 8. Example of the resulting map data

calculated for the user. The second type oftable (Table 2)saves all the positions calculated and the time that the localization was made. This way we have all the positions
of the user for future behavior analysis. We can recreate the path that the user took or
the place where the user stood still, or other requirements that the application needs.

Table 2. Example of user data stored internally

SavedLocation Id	User Id	Latitude	Longitude	Hour
0	1	40.19237°	-8.414629°	hour
1	1	40.192378°	-8.414513°	hour
2	1	40.192384°	-8.414381°	hour
3	1	40.192389°	-8.414227°	hour
4	1	40.192356°	-8.414132°	hour

8   Exploring the Technology

The current version of the system relies on a localization server to hostall the data and
the localization fingerprinting processing, which results in a very light client. This
client can easily be refactored as an API (Application Programming Interface) to be
integrated in other applications with the only requirement of access to the device received wireless broadcast beacons. On a server side, the stored user information can
be used for integration with existing health and other user information based systems.
An integration in such a system is easily possible, as the universal web service interface can be easily expanded to fit any web based platform, and therefore with the
needs of any AAL application.

An older version of the system works exclusively offline, with all the necessary data and processing being done on the client side. This has a considerably larger load on
the client application, with all the data and processing being local. The required data
can either be created locally, by creating a new set of floor plans and calibrations; or it

can be acquired bya single download online. This solution has the advantage of not requiring a constant network connection, but has considerable requirements on the data access, user procedures and processing power, which result in a high barrier to entry and low battery life on the mobile devices. It also exposes some of the key technologies IP (Intellectual Property) of the system in a managed programming language, which is easily decompiled.

8.1   Performance Evaluation

In order to assess the objective accuracy of the localization system, an evaluation session was performed under semi-controlled environment. 15 calibration points were recorded to the system (as seen in Fig. 9), in positions throughout one floor, from one end of the building to the other. These will be the reference points that the system should predict if you're on or near them. The system guidelines indicate the calibration should be done in typical final user usage fashion. As such and for the purpose of a reliable test, the Android devices were positioned using a static holder, avoiding the interference of the human operator, both in calibration and localization.

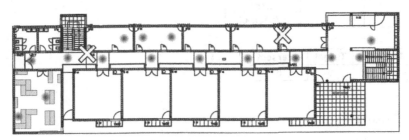

Fig. 9. Reference calibrated points

Due to time constraints, only 6 randomly selected locations were tested, each with at least 3 minutes sampling time. During the calibration and localization, several real-world factors influenced the system, including:

- Varying temperature and humidity throughout a day
- Access point concurrency collision
- Multiple wireless clients connected to access points
- Target devices maintained a roaming connection to the local wireless network to access the location server
- People walking across the building
- Target devices heated up due to continuous usage

The system must be able to cope to such changes without much precision loss, thus the tests we actually performed in a very close to a real-word scenario.

The results were logged in files, on for each sample and compiled for analysis. The error metric used was absolute Geodesic degrees which indicated a hit or miss, if the resulting error was zero.

The resulting data set (Table 3) shows the errors and sample sizes, consisting of sample descriptions, where the resulting absolute error is presented in World Geodetic System (WGS84) decimal degrees. The hit/intersect results F-Assessment, used for the F-Measure [3] calculation are also presented. The F-Measure results, where precision and recall are the quotient from the matched localization on the unmatched or false positives.

Table 3. Resulting performance analysis data

Sample	Sample size	Absolute error
1	7	3,55935E-05
2	10	3,91151E-05
3	11	3,4289E-05
4	9	2,8342E-05
5	15	2,66877E-05
6	11	2,85057E-06
	63	
		Average error
		2,7813E-05

Precision	0,375
Recall	1
True negative rate	0
Accuracy	0,375
F	0,545454545

Measured	Target	Intersect
16	6	6

9   Future Work

The indoor localization systems based on Wi-Fi have some limitations in terms of accuracy, but enough for fulfill the requirements of the target systems. However, by combining this system with other technologies will improve the results.

In Figure 10 we can see how the direction of the user is facing can influence the signal strength on the device [2].

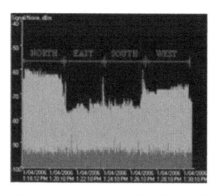

Fig. 10. Example of varying signal strengthwith different directionsof the user

Our solution has just one simple type of calibration. We will improve this technique with several calibrations with different aspects that will personalize the signals for each utilization. If the user is holding the device upside down, or sideways, during the calibration process, the information will be saved. Later while the localization is performed, the algorithm will take in consideration how the device is positioned to choose between the different calibrations made.

With these two improvements of new types of calibration and new sensors information we will get a more confident result, and then we will concentrate our efforts in a new method to display the position of the user. It will be made a representation of the user positions in 3D to be accessible through a web browser using HTML5.

Acknowledgements. The work described here was supported by the Co-Living project, which is funded by the Ambient Assisted Living (AAL) Joint Programme (contract n° AAL-2009-2-097) and the national funding authorities of The Netherlands, Norway, Cyprus, Portugal, and Spain.

References

1. Quintas, J., Charalambous, Y., Tsiourti, C., Dias, J.: Integration of an Automatic Indoor and Outdoor Activity Monitoring with a Social Network. JAPA Supplement 20(suppl.) (August 2012)
2. Dempster, A.G., Li, B., Quader, I.: Errors in Determinstic Wireless Fingerprinting Systems for Localisation (2008)
3. Van Rijsbergen, C.J.: Information Retrieval. Butterworths (1979)
4. Piché, R.: Location Fingerprinting methods in wireless local area networks. Master of Science Thesis. Faculty of Science and Environmental Engineering, pp. 1–93 (2008)

Indoor Localization Based on Resonant Oscillating Magnetic Fields for AAL Applications

Gerald Pirkl and Paul Lukowicz

Embedded Intelligence
DFKI GmbH Kaiserslautern, Technical University of Kaiserslautern, Germany

Abstract. Building the basic concept of a low cost, robust, indoor positioning system based on magnetic resonant coupling that we have presented in previous work we describe our entry into the EVAAL indoor location competition. The basic physical principle behind the system makes it extremely robust as the signals are hardly influenced by the human body or objects in the environment (except massive metal objects which however have mostly local influence only). Going beyond previous work we provide a detailed description of the processing architecture, show how the system can be set up on the basis of the floor-plan alone (no location specific training or measurements needed), present the software tools that can be used for system setup and application and evaluate floor plan based setup looking specifically into the influence of multiple people and changes in furniture configuration.

Keywords: Indoor Localization, Resonant Oscillating Magnetic Coupling, Software Architecture, Particle Filter.

1 Introduction

There has been tremendous progress in indoor positioning technology over recent years. Approaches range from leveraging inertial sensors in smart phones to elaborate, dedicated infrastructure such as RF beacons or floor integrated sensors and include sophisticated methods for considering background information (e.g. building plans) and fusion of different sensing modalities. However, for many applications, there is still no technology that satisfies all requirement. In this paper we focus on the requirements of activity recognition in Ambient Assisted Living applications. For such applications the following key properties are important:

1. Positioning accuracy in the range of around 1m. This allows the system to distinguish basic activity relevant "symbolic locations" such as for example "in front of the refrigerator", "at the table", "on the sofa" or "in front of the pills cabinet". Many current systems, in particular cheap and easily deployable ones such as WiFi location are not able to reliably achieve such accuracy.
2. Ability to deal with dynamic and cluttered environments. Thus, the system should not be influenced by people moving around, doors being open or furniture being moved. Again, many cheap and easily deployable systems have difficulties.
3. Low cost and most of all easy deployment. Cost of more than a few hundred Euro and/or require complex installation (e.g. embedding sensors or RFIDs in the floor or elaborate location specific training) are among the key obstacles for wide scale deployment of AAL systems.

J.A. Botía et al. (Eds.): EvAAL 2013, CCIS 386, pp. 128–140, 2013.

In [9] we have presented the basic concept of a low cost, robust, indoor positioning system based on magnetic resonant coupling that can achieve an accuracy of well below 1m. In this paper we describe our entry into the EVAAL indoor location competition that is based on this concept. Going beyond [9] we provide a detailed description of the processing architecture, show how the system can be set up on the basis of the floorplan alone (no location specific training or measurements needed), present the software tools that can be used for system setup and application and evaluate floor plan based setup looking specifically into the influence of multiple people and changes in furniture configuration. Furthermore the current version of the system includes additional acceleration and gyroscope sensors which are used as input to a filter stabilizing the location estimate.

The system is built around 3D transmitter coils (16x16x16 cm) and receiver coils (2x2x2 cm) operating in TDMA mode. A **single** 3D transmitter coil can cover an area with 8m diameter providing 3D position for the receiver badges with an accuracy below $1m^2$ and an update rate of up to 30Hz. Higher accuracies can be achieved by combining information from several transmitter coils. The basic physical principle behind the system (which is well known and has been used before for motion tracking, power transmission, or near field communication) makes it extremely robust as the signals are hardly influenced by the human body or objects in the environment (except massive metal objects which however have mostly local influence only).

1.1 Related Work

Giving an overview of research in indoor localization is clearly beyond the scope of this paper (see for example [6] or [13]). On a technical level most closely related to our system are beacon based technologies that compute user position from signal strength or signal delay to/from several (at least 3) beacons. This includes ultrasound based systems like Cricket [11] or Active Bat [15] and infrared (Ir) light such the Active Badge by Want et al. [14], all based on time of flight measurements. The main disadvantages of these systems are multi path and occlusion problems and the need to deploy at least three appropriately distributed devices in every room (since the signal is blocked by walls). Occlusion and multi path propagation are less of an issue with signal strength based radio frequency (RF) systems for example based on WiFi infrastructure (e.g. [2] or [1]. However such system require elaborate fingerprinting of specific locations and are in general very sensitive to dynamic changes in the environment. The accuracy is in general well above 1m. An RF indoor localization system which is often used for applications requiring high accuracy (see for example health care applications like presented in [4]) is the Ubisense system. Time-difference-of-arrival and angle-of-arrival estimation between stationary receiver antennas allow a position estimation within an accuracy of 30 cm. However, metal objects like table frames or door frames interfere with the ultra wide band pulse and significantly disturb the position estimation process. Other issues are the high costs of the system and the high installation and calibration effort.

Aiming at lower installation effort Patel et al. [12] presented a system that uses power line installations as ultra wide band antennas and finger printing and achieves an accuracy 1 m^2. The main limitation is the limited range which requires the user to be close to a power line. The use of magnetic fields for indoor location similar to this work has been explored by Prigge et al. [10]. However, whereas our system is based on highly energy efficient resonant coupling to filter out other magnetic fields, theirs uses a CDMA coding scheme in a non resonant mode. According to the authors the system needs about 100 W per Beacon and requires cables running between the Beacons for synchronization. Our system, on the other hand, uses only 2.5W per Beacon and relies on RF time synchronization (needing no cables). Furthermore, we use 3D transmitters which means that we can get rough localization with just one transmitter, whereas the Prigge setup requires at least 3.

The underlying physical principle of resonant magnetic coupling is well known and has been used in many different applications. This includes motion tracking [3], wireless power transmission has been presented in [5], track the lives of underground animals, [7] and novel user interfaces for musical instruments . [8].

2   General Principle

In this section we summarize the physical principle behind our system that is described and discussed in more detail in [9].

2.1   Properties of Oscillating Magnetic Fields

Our system is based on the principle of resonant magnetic coupling, which means that it uses an oscillating magnetic field as the physical medium for localization. Thus, our beacons generate a magnetic field that periodically expands and contracts (Figure 1). Note that there is a fundamental difference with respect to for example RF or ultrasonic beacons which both generate propagating waves. By contrast the magnetic field in our system does not separate from the transmitter and propagate. Instead the vast majority of energy is "pulled back" into the oscillating circuit as the field contracts. The above

Fig. 1. Expansion and contraction of the oscillating magnetic field

principle has a number of advantages. First of all since nothing propagates and there are no waves multi path propagation, reflections, diffraction do not occur. Furthermore, magnetic fields are inherently difficult to block. They pass with little distortion through most materials including human tissue and concrete walls. Only ferromagnetic materials and conductors have an influence. However, even massive metal objects do not block the signal but have mostly local influence. While the influence of ferromagnetic objects on the field can be complex, on an abstract level it can be described as bending the field lines *running within the object*. To match the bending inside the object the field lines outside are also deformed but to a lesser degree and mostly in the proximity of the object. Thus we only see an effect if the object is close to the receiver or (to a lesser extent) to the transmitter. Unlike with RF systems the mere presence of the object in the vicinity has virtually no effect. This means that there is no need for finger printing to account for the specific configuration of furniture, walls etc.

2.2 Location Principle

Magnetic field is often visualized by field lines. In a 2 D representation a field line is a curve through space drawn in such a way that all points on the curve have the same field strength. In 3D lines become surfaces. If we look at the field of a single transmitter coil then a single measurement restricts set of possible locations to a single surface. If we add another coil then the set of possible locations is narrowed down to the intersection of two surfaces. Adding yet another coil further restricts the locations to a set of points at the intersection of the three surfaces (see Figure 3). This is very similar to the well known principle of triangulation used in most beacon based positioning systems. The main difference stems from the fact that if we use perpendicular coils then we can put them all in the same location instead of having to distribute them at different spatial locations. This is due to the non spherical structure of the magnetic field of a typical coils as shown in figures 1 and figure 2. This means that using three perpendicular transmitter coils placed at a *single location* allows the receiver position to be restricted to a few points given by the symmetry of the magnetic field. Exact 3D positioning is possible with two beacon nodes. Note that the above assumes the transmitter coils to be synchronized to transmit after each other to avoid an overlap of their fields.

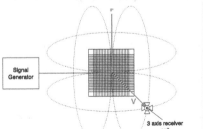 

Fig. 2. Left: The transmitter sequentially generates an oscillating magnetic field in a certain frequency interval with three perpendicular transmitter coils. The three perpendicular receiver coils measure the induced voltage of the magnetic field. Right: Cubes are two versions of transmitter coils, in the front the wearable receiver and the stationary and wearable transmitter part.

2.3 Orientation Effects

In the above discussion we have assumed a scalar value of the magnetic field strength to be measured at any given point. However the magnetic field is a vector field. Thus, each measurement needs to encompass the 3 vector components m_x, m_y, m_z from which the scalar vector norm can be computed as $\sqrt{m_x^2 + m_y^2 + m_z^2}$.

The simplest way to measure the three components is to equip the receiver with three perpendicular coils. Note that we have outlined above that the transmitter needs at least 3 perpendicular coils. With the 3 receiver coils we now have 9 measurements in that have to be made for position estimation: the signal. Thus the signal of each transmitter coil is measured by each of the three receiver coils. For each transmitter coil the three measurements can be used to estimate the scalar field norm and with it the set of points to which the receiver location can be constrained. The field direction can then be used in one of two possible ways. If we know the absolute orientation of the receiver then it can be used to narrow the location down to a single point (in general at each intersection of the field line surfaces the field direction is different.). On the other hand if we already know the exact point (e.g. through tracking or through the use of additional transmitters, then this information can be used to infer the relative orientation of the receiver with respect to the transmitter.

2.4 Resonant Coupling

A key concern with any indoor magnetic measurement system is noise caused by electrical appliance and other environmental fields. To address this concern our system uses the principle of narrow frequency resonant coupling. A transmitter generates an oscillating magnetic field with a well defined narrow frequency. The field excites a receiver which is essentially an oscillating circuit precisely tuned to the respective frequency. The strength of the excitation (=induced voltage) depends on the location of the receiver in the transmitter field, which is the basic effect that we use for positioning as described above. Due to the narrow resonant frequency the system is robust against

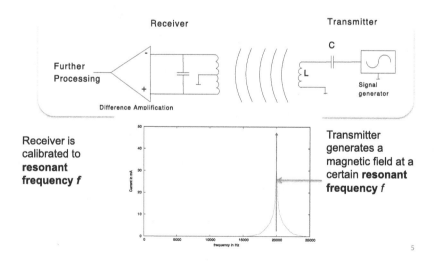

Fig. 3. Oscillating circuits included in the transmitter and receiver coils filter out influences of other electro magnetic sources and maximize the power output of the transmitter coils. The lower signal plot depicts the sensitivity of the receiver coil linked to the frequency of the magnetic field.

environmental magnetic fields. Only fields with that exactly match the resonant frequency can disturb the measurement, which (with properly chosen frequency) is highly unlikely. At the same time narrow frequency oscillations are unlikely to couple to any environmental devices.

2.5 Summary

In summary, because of the underlying physical principle, magnetic resonant coupling technology is much less sensitive to disturbance typically found in indoor environments. Because of the structure of the field a single beacon only is needed for a basic position estimate and the signal even contains information about receiver orientation.

On the negative side there are a number of complex problems that need to be solved such as very large dynamic range of the signal (the energy transmitted in the field decreases with $1/r^6$), the difficulty of handling the need for a very narrow resonant range (mostly due to manufacturing tolerances of standard components), and the difficulty in accurate modeling of the magnetic field (the exact form of the field line surfaces). How we have approached these problems has been discussed in [9] and will not be further elaborated in this paper.

3 Oscillating Magnetic Field Sensor System

In this section we describe the functionality of the hard- and software.

3.1 Hardware Overview

Our system consists of two parts: Field emitters and wearable field receivers. The magnetic field transmitter generates magnetic fields using 3 perpendicular transmission coils (200 turns, 16 cm × 16 cm). Each coil is sequentially excited using a 16V peak to peak square shaped input signal at a current of 0.17A. To maximize the power output of the magnetic field an oscillating circuit is connected to the coil. To overcome hardware tolerances (timing / frequency issues on the signal generator, temperature effects and therefore mistuning of the oscillating circuit) we use the so called wobbling mechanism, the coil is not excited with a fixed frequency but we apply different frequencies in the interval of $[18.5kHz; 21.5kHz]$.

On the receiver side a 3D receiver coil measures the magnetic field at its position. The induced voltage is filtered by an oscillating circuit, electromagnetic sources have hardly any effects on the induced voltage. A combination of differential and programmable / adjustable amplifiers enable the system to deal with the high dynamic input signal (1.5V at 20 cm, 0.004V at 4 m). In addition to the magnetic field system, gyroscope and acceleration sensors are also sampled. The data is transferred using a serial connection to the computer or a Zigbee based RF Connection. A on board micro SD card can also be used to store the data for offline data processing. Using a LiPo battery, the sensor receiver works for 8 hours, due to its current prototype state no battery saving mechanisms are installed to increase the uptime of the system.

3.2   Software Architecture

The used software architecture is divided into two parts, a component running on the Microchip DsPic and a software component running on the PC. The transmitter software is mainly controlling the signal generator part, some sensor network tasks like time synchronisation or scheduling is organised on these network nodes. The more interesting part is located on the receiver where we have to control the sampling of the magnetic field signal.

An overview of both , the receiver part and the PC software part for position estimation is depicted in figure 4.

Embedded Software on Receiver. The software on the receiver is mainly gathering the magnetic field information. To sample the data it is necessary to strictly time synchronize all clocks of the transmitters and receivers using an RF based time synchronisation process. The synchronized real time clock fires every 2.5 ms which indicates the start of a processing frame. A sampling cycle consists of 5 frames, the first 3 frames are used to sample the 3 sequentially generated magnetic fields of the current transmitter, in the other frames the micro controller processes the data, transfers data to the pc (using RF or cable bound communication) and performs sensor network tasks (like time synchronisation or scheduling algorithms). While being in the sampling state the micro controller samples the input voltage of the receiver coils with a sampling rate of 80kHz for 1.6ms. This time value is the best trade off between on-board memory consumption

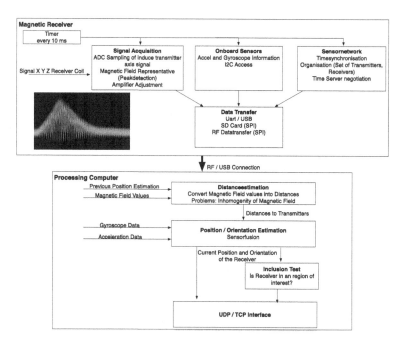

Fig. 4. Processing Architecture of the Magnetic field based localization system

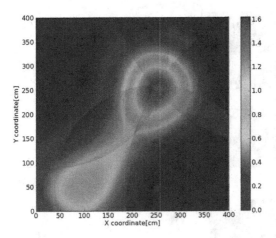

Fig. 5. Estimated particle weights, random transmitter positions, measurement distances are derived from the point (250,250,80). The green circles depict the used distances, the green squares the transmitters.

of the DMA buffers on the micro controller and the time the circuits need to respond to the magnetic field excitement. The controller then uses a peak detection algorithm on the full buffers. In order to stabilize the signal, the controller uses the mean value of all peaks which are in the interval of $[0.9 * maxPeak; maxPeak]$ to distinguish the magnetic field representative. After processing is done the magnetic raw values are used to adjust the amplifier values in order to maximize the resolution of the sensor system.

In addition to the magnetic sensor part, gyroscope and acceleration sensors are sampled, this information is transferred to the processing computer for sensor data fusion, sensor orientation estimation and signal filtering.

Position and Orientation Estimation on PC. Data processing is done on a PC because of the limited ressources of the microcontroller on the magnetic receiver. Processing and filtering is written in Python, all visual elements are implemented in a Java based application with a network interface to listen to magnetic localization information broadcasts.

After retrieving the magnetic field data from the serial connection, the information is transformed into distance values. In this step the magnetic field behaviour (described by the law of Biot Savart) and the inhomogeneity of the magnetic field have been taken into account to increase the accuracy of the distance estimation. A particle filter estimates the position of the receiver, it fuses gyroscope and acceleration information for a more accurate position and orientation estimation. A single particle described by the tuple $(x, y, z, \rho, \phi, \theta)$ represents a possible position and orientation (heading/yaw, roll and pitch) of the receiver. A measurement is a tuple $(d1, ..., dn, \rho, \phi, \theta)$ where d_i defines the estimated distances between the transmitters t_i and the receiver, ρ, ϕ, θ describe the orientation estimation derived from the acceleration and gyroscope information.

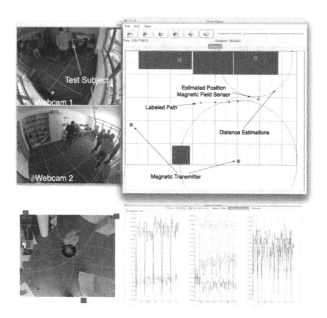

Fig. 6. Screenshot of the *MagSys* application, on the left hand side two different webcams recorded the scene from different directions, on the right hand side a schematic view on the room, the locations of the sensor components, sensor data and the possibility to annotate the position of persons and devices

In order to weight a particle we calculate for each particle the distance to transmitter i and compare this value with the measurement:

$\epsilon_i = \frac{d_i - ||\mathbf{t_i} - \mathbf{p}||}{d_i}$ describes the distance error for the measurement of transmitter i.

The error value ϵ_i is then statistically evaluated using a gaussian distribution (this takes the mean error and standard deviation of the distance estimation derived from a calibration process into account). The weight of a particle is therefore:

$$w(p) = \prod_{i=0}^{n} norm(\epsilon_i, \mu, \sigma)$$

After the measurement step, the particles are moved according to the heading and speed information (plus a Gausian noise value). The estimated position is then presented to the magnetic field model to flatten the effects of the inhomogeneity of the magnetic field and to the inclusion module which tests if the position is in a region of interest.

Each module is attached to the network module which broadcasts this information to the network. The user can therefore decide which information is important (Raw sensor information, intermediate data or high level data as "user is next to the TV").

3.3 Highlevel Userinterfaces

We implemented a Java based application *MagSys* which can be used to retrieve the information transmitted in the lower level position estimation program presented in the previous subsection. The application encapsulates several components linked to the functions of the magnetic indoor localization system but due to the simple interfaces of the GUI Components, new sensors can easily be integrated. The main functions are:

1. Calibration and setup of the localization system
2. Definition of region of interests
3. On- / off line illustration of the sensor data (current position, meta information like "receiver is in a region of interest", on-line annotation of activites and positions, sensor data)
4. Integration of network cameras for ground truth information (online dewarping of fisheye webcam pictures)
5. Off-line annotation and replay functionality of recorded data sets for post processing
6. Simple integration of new sensor modalities (especially Beacon based sensorsystems)

MagSys' core functionality is the sketching mechanism to draw experiment setups. Floors with rooms and furniture can be specified and integrated in the experiment setup. Stationary sensor systems as the magnetic field indoor localization system are easily integrated and can be configured and calibrated with this tool. *MagSys* connects to the LAN and displays sensor information from the localization system. As depicted in the upper part of figure 6 distance and position information are included in the room sketch. Network based cameras can also be intregated, an OpenCV based diswarping function removes lense distortions and therefore combine localization data with camera information (figure 6 lower left part) to surveil the experiment in real time. Raw sensor information from the magnetic field sensor, accelerometers and gyroscope can be watched in different sections of the program to ensure the correct functionality of the system. *MagSys* also supports the offline processing and annotation of position based experiments, the experimenter can load webcam images and sensor data and annotate the correct position according to the webcam supported scenes on a frame by frame basis.

4   Evaluation

Our previous work [9] where we distinguished between up to 20 different region of interests in a typical living area has been improved, we transform the raw magnetic values into Cartesian coordinates and evaluate the estimated positions against video based and manually annotated groundtruth position information.

In addition to the accuracy of the system we want to show the robustness against obstacles (ferromagnetic materials and furniture) or persons working in the covered area.

Four transmitters have been spread in a 37 m^2 room (7.7 m × 4.9 m). To show the robustness of our system, in particular its functionality when there is no direct line of sight between the field emitter and the receiver, a transmitter is placed in a cabinet with ferromagnetic shelves and closed cabinet doors, a second transmitter is placed above a bookshelf. For these two transmitter in most positions of the room no direct line of sight is available, the magnetic field has to permeate furniture or even persons. We evaluate the system in three steps, the prerequisites are the same for all experiments: The test subject carries the receiver unit attached to the belt (height approx. 80cm), and randomly walks in the room. During the walk, we record the measured magnetic field strengths with a sampling rate of 20 Hz (20 position estimations per second). Two fish eye cameras record the scenes from two different spots.

To prove our assumptions that the magnetic field is hardly influenced by persons, furniture or ferromagnetic material, three steps are made: Data recording in

1. an empty room (see figure 7 for details)
2. the same room but with static obstacles which would alter electro magnetic fields or change the propagation behaviour of electro magnetic waves. We therefore place furniture and metal tripods in the center of the room and add a 1.5 m^2 big metal white board next to transmitter 4
3. the same room with 7 persons randomly strolling around in the room (dynamic environment).

A trial takes about 10 minutes, we record the raw magnetic field values measured at the receiver's position, two webcams surveilling the room record the scene for later manual position annotation (see section 3.3).

Processing and Results. After manually annotating the positions of the receiver we compare the positions estimated by our magnetic field system with the real life coordinates.

Table 1.

Exp number	absolute mean position error	std	length
1	60.32	39.05	241.2m
2	54.24	38.2	178.8m
3	62.63	41.2	235.7m

Fig. 7. a) Room with obstacles in the center, b) empty room setup with test subject c) room with 7 persons randomly walking around d) schematic room setup with transmitter coils (orange squares)

Table 1 holds the accuracies we currently achieve in 3D position estimation. Experiment 2, where we placed obstacles in the center of the room, has a higher accuracy as the other two experiments. This phenomenon results from the currently used distance model: due to the physical behaviour of the magnetic field (and therefore the $\frac{1}{d^3}$ drop of the signal), the accuracy of the distance estimation decreases with rising distance (in the real world). In Experiment 2 we block the area in the center of the room, a region where the distances to the transmitters are more inaccurate compared to outer room regions and therefore the performance of the positioning is poor. When excluding this area in the other two experiments, the accuracy rises in experiment 1 (the empty room) from 60.32 to 56.64 and in experiment 3 from 62.63 to 58.3. The standard deviations of these experiments are hardly affected.

5   Conclusion

The system described in this paper is aimed at robust, cheap and easily deployable indoor location with an accuracy of below 1m. Within the AAL context robust means that the system is not significantly disturbed by change in the environment such as people moving around, doors being opened or furniture being rearranged. Easily deployable means that, installing the system at a new location amounts to placing on average one transmitter per room and noting the location of the transmitter on a plan of the flat using our tools. There is no need for location specific training. Furthermore the transmitters do not need line of site to the receivers carried by the users and can be placed out of sight e.g. in cabinets.

Acknowledgment. This work has been supported by the German Federal Ministry of Education and Research (BMBF) under Project Number 01IW12002 CoCoRec.

References

1. LaMarca, A., et al.: Place lab: Device positioning using radio beacons in the wild. In: Gellersen, H.-W., Want, R., Schmidt, A. (eds.) PERVASIVE 2005. LNCS, vol. 3468, pp. 116–133. Springer, Heidelberg (2005)
2. Bahl, P., Padmanabhan, V.N.: RADAR: An in-building RF-based user location and tracking system. In: IEEE International Conference on Computer Communications (2), pp. 775–784 (2000)
3. Hamaguchi, A., Kanbara, M., Yokoya, N.: User localization using wearable electromagnetic tracker and orientation sensor. In: 10th IEEE International Symposium on Wearable Computers, pp. 55–58 (October 2006)
4. Hanser, F., Gruenerbl, A., Rodegast, C., Lukowicz, P.: Design and real life deployment of a pervasive monitoring system for dementia patients. In: Second International Conference on Pervasive Computing Technologies for Healthcare (2008)
5. Kurs, A., Karalis, A., Moffatt, R., Joannopoulos, J.D., Fisher, P., Soljačić, M.: Wireless power transfer via strongly coupled magnetic resonances. Science 317(5834), 83–86 (2007)
6. Liu, H., Darabi, H., Banerjee, P., Liu, J.: Survey of wireless indoor positioning techniques and systems. IEEE Transactions on Systems, Man and Cybernetics, Part C: Applications and Reviews 37(6), 1067–1080 (2007)

7. Markham, A., Trigoni, N., Ellwood, S.A., Macdonald, D.W.: Revealing the hidden lives of underground animals using magneto-inductive tracking. In: Proceedings of the 8th ACM Conference on Embedded Networked Sensor Systems, SenSys 2010, pp. 281–294. ACM, New York (2010)
8. Paradiso, J.A., Hsiao, K.-Y., Benbasat, A.: Tangible music interfaces using passive magnetic tags. In: Proceedings of the 2001 Conference on New Interfaces for Musical Expression, NIME 2001, pp. 1–4. National University of Singapore, Singapore (2001)
9. Pirkl, G., Lukowicz, P.: Robust, low cost indoor positioning using magnetic resonant coupling. In: Proceedings of the 2012 ACM Conference on Ubiquitous Computing, pp. 431–440. ACM (2012)
10. Prigge, E.A., How, J.P.: Signal architecture for a distributed magnetic local positioning system. IEEE Sensors Journal 4(6), 864–873 (2004)
11. Priyantha, N.B., Chakraborty, A., Balakrishnan, H.: The Cricket Location-Support System. In: 6th ACM International Conference on Mobile Computing and Networking, Boston, MA (August 2000)
12. Stuntebeck, E.P., Patel, S.N., Robertson, T., Reynolds, M.S., Abowd, G.D.: Wideband powerline positioning for indoor localization. In: International Conference on Ubiquitous Computing, pp. 94–103 (2008)
13. Torres-solis, J., Falk, T.H., Chau, T.: A review of indoor localization technologies: towards navigational assistance for topographical disorientation. In: Ambient Intelligence, pp. 51–84 (2010)
14. Want, R., Hopper, A., Falcão, V., Gibbons, J.: The active badge location system. ACM Transactions on Information Systems 10(1), 91–102 (1992)
15. Ward, A., Jones, A., Hopper, A.: A new location technique for the active office. IEEE Personal Communications 4, 42–47 (1997)

Author Index